MYTHS, LIES, AND MERCY

MYTHS, LIES, AND MERCY

Exposing the forces that perpetuate & criminalize homelessness

EDDIE YOUNG

Disrupted Life Publishing

ISBN 9780578291451

CONTENTS

For

Guerry Patton
"Chattanooga"

I miss your voice

Preface

I first came across the concept of street newspapers while living in Scotland. Walking through the city centre, I'd see a person once in a while selling papers, and they didn't appear to be your typical news or city papers, so I looked closer. *The Big Issue.* At the time, I was a minister in the Christian faith and had accepted a request to come and work with a small inner-city church. We met in an abandoned shop in a small square within a block of council housing flats. The poverty among those living there disrupted the trajectory of my life and my thoughts on life. If they were living in the States, they would all most certainly be homeless. But Britain has safety nets. Running into a homeless person was rare, and so I was drawn to this man selling these papers. I didn't conclude he was homeless by his looks, but he did have the appearance of someone whose life had been beaten down. I bought a paper from him, sat down for a coffee, and became absorbed in the shameful truths about homelessness and the personal stories that were told.

When I returned to the States, homelessness was everywhere. It had always been everywhere, but I had been both ignorant to this big issue, and a stranger to those living in it. I immersed myself into an advocacy position, and then into organizing the homeless community to pursue solution-based dialogue with the stakeholders of the city. In addition to the work of our Homeless Collective, I launched a street newspaper to amplify the voices of those behind the issue. For there to ever be any change, minds have to change. Along the way, I try to be very intentional about my patience for those who've never been exposed to the truths that perpetuate and even create homelessness. Until given an alternative perspective, it's understandable that people will assume to be true what they've always been told is true. I have no patience at all, however, for those who do and or should know better. People in power, neighborhood and business associations, law enforcement, elected officials, and yes, even some service providers, who pedal myths and lies in order to secure votes, justify their deplorable actions, assuage their guilt, and to keep their shelters in business. It's these whose minds must be changed, and that has been and will continue to be a formidable task.

This collection of editorials exposes the myths and lies while offering an alternative perspective with hopes of inspiring to fuel action, and equipping to affect change.

An Everlasting Now

I was having lunch in a local restaurant and discussing the work that we do with a couple of friends, all the while noticing that someone seated nearby at the bar was listening in on our conversation. This gentleman had apparently heard enough and so he leans over to our table, and interrupting with a smile of condescension, assured me that "most of the homeless choose to live that way." Managing somehow to control and suppress my indignation for such an ignorant and unfounded assertion, I rejoined my friends in conversation after assuring this gentleman that it is extremely rare to find someone who has actually "chosen" to live without the security and stability of a home. Closer to the truth is that many of the homeless across our communities have come to embrace their hopelessness – they've lost all trust in the systems that at best do not work for them, and at worst intentionally push and/or keep them beyond the margins of society.

The demeanor that those in the mainstream witness and mistakenly attribute to evidence that they have chosen this lifestyle, is most often an expression of the ways in which they attempt to cope with a bitter and empty existence. At some point, it is understandable how someone might choose to give up trying. As a community in a sports culture stupor, we can understand this. Imagine how demoralizing it is to go into the fourth quarter of a football game trailing 52-0. Your coach is telling you, "Don't give up! The game's not over." Well, he's right, technically it's not over but for all practical purposes, it is. And the players know it. How long do you continue to give your all for what you believe is a losing cause, embrace the reality and settle into going through the motions?

Comments like, "They choose to live that way" not only add heartless insult to injury for those living in desperate poverty, (maybe one of the benefits to not living shoulder to shoulder with those of us in more privileged positions is that they're not close enough to us to hear thoughtless comments like this), but they also serve to assuage the consciences of those who make them. Operating on the premise that those who are living in poverty and homelessness have chosen that lifestyle makes us feel better about the society that we help to create and promote. And of course, if we were to acknowledge that someone has actually fallen victim to circumstances beyond their control, we insert our belief that anyone can "pull themselves up by their bootstraps."

But what if?

What if, and I know there are some – very few, but some, there *are* people who have chosen this lifestyle? Or maybe not chosen this lifestyle as much as *not* chosen the lifestyle that the rest of us have? Jan Yoors at the age of twelve ran away from home in 1934 to join a Gypsy *kumpania*, the *Romanies,* and lived among them for ten years. Yoors observed that "The Gypsies, seemingly immune to progress, live in an everlasting Now, in a perpetual, heroic present, as if thy recognized only the slow pulse of eternity and were content to live in the margin of history... they're social organization is forever fluid, yet has an internal vitality." What if those romantic words were to describe some of the homeless who share this city with us? Is it possible that some of our disdain for them can better be attributed to our envying their courage in choosing the simplicity of the lifestyle that they live? Would any of us dare to admit to this? Probably not. Most of us will get up in the morning and engage once again in what we admittedly refer to as the "rat race." Some of us sitting at a desk and dreaming of a simpler life – living in an "everlasting Now" but bound by the obligations of an existence that has all the meaningfulness of treading water – going nowhere and working ourselves to exhaustion to stay afloat yet affirming that it's the right thing to do because it's just what people do

There really aren't many people experiencing homelessness in our midst who can be described as grasping for life in an "everlasting Now" (choosing a life of homelessness), that's a myth. But the few that you do come across can be challenging to one's perspectives on the approach to life. They make one think and wonder, (if there's space in our busy schedule), and usually, all they ask in return is a little change, something to keep them warm, and a little food to eat.

I'm ok with that.

Love Mercy, But Act With Justice

I just read through Robert Lupton's *Toxic Charity*, a book that's been making it's rounds lately, mainly among faith-based organizations. I must take issue with, in particular, his explanation of the prophet Micah's call to act with justice and love mercy. Because his understanding of this text appears to be the foundation upon which he builds his approach in working among the poor, it would be crucial to his argument that he get it right.

To begin, Lupton makes the mistake of defining mercy as "a force that compels us to acts of compassion." This is confusing and simply not correct; he actually has it backwards. Mercy is not a force; it is the act. Compassion comes closer to being defined as a force. For example, compassion is the deep-seated feeling that Jesus had (it is described as dwelling in his very bowels) for the oppressed crowds that drove him to acts of mercy. But one can have feelings of compassion without ever engaging in a show of mercy; it happens every day (just as one can extend acts of mercy that are not driven by feelings of compassion). My point is this:

Micah is appealing to a directive from God that says "act." One cannot be blamed for a lack of compassion; the feeling is either stirred or it isn't. You can't create it upon command. You *can* act however, and this is what Micah says to love – love mercy. According to Micah, God gives no directives on our love for feelings – compassion. He wants us to love acts – mercy.

When it comes to justice, Lupton is at least partly right when he says that "justice without mercy is cold and impersonal, more concerned about rights than relationships." Well, justice is very concerned with the pursuit of and the protection of one's rights – whether an individual or a population. It has to do with setting things right – balancing the scales. And what does Micah say? Do this. But Lupton is claiming that acts of justice and acts of mercy are an inseparable pair. Each is useless, and even deadly, without the other. I'm not sure how that claim is deduced unless it has to do with them appearing together in the same sentence. He's all over the place here. First, he continues to treat mercy as a force, without which justice is "cold and impersonal." And it is here that he shows his hand. He's trying his best to tie these two together in order to support the premise of his book, that mercy without justice, (the thing he will define as justice) is a dose of poison – that when these two are "divorced, they become deformed." But then he shifts and begins describing mercy as an act, one that without justice, "degenerates (one) into dependency and entitlement..." And we can all see where this is going.

Lupton defines justice above as actions concerned with rights, but then it immediately disappears into a new definition, the one he wants to operate from – the intentional move "in the direction of development." It's hard to figure out how Lupton squares this with Micah's idea of justice, but based on the logic of his reasoning, somehow the idea of justice is wrapped up and found in his following axioms:

Immediate care (mercy) with *a future plan (justice).*
Emergency relief (mercy) and *responsible development (justice).*
short-term intervention (mercy) and *long-term involvement (justice).*
Heart responses (mercy) and *engaged minds (justice).*

The idea is that acts of mercy are "irresponsible" if not coupled with developmental work. He actually says, "What good is a sandwich and a cup of soup when a severe addiction has control of a man's life?" In regard to food banks, he asks, "Why do we persist in giving away food when we *know* it fosters dependency?"

Here Lupton strays from Micah's directives. Developmental work among the poor is hugely important, but it is not what Micah is saying. The truth is, if you take the idea of justice as Micah intends it, doing developmental work becomes infinitely more doable. We are not only to be concerned with acting justly with one another on a personal level but creating systems that operate justly and changing those that don't. Again, developmental work among the poor is crucial, but you can't define it as "justice," put it on Micah's lips, couple it inseparably with "mercy" and conclude that one without the other is "toxic."

Underlying this conclusion, and the spirit that I see throughout the book, if not stated clearly and unashamedly, is that you should only show mercy to those who deserve it. And it is here where Lupton fully and completely departs from Micah's directives. Micah attaches no qualifications to the recipients of our mercy. It's as though he were saying, "If you had rain to mercifully give, it'd be okay to make it fall on the just *and* the unjust, (See Jesus of Nazareth, Sermon on the Mount).

But according to Lupton, that would be spreading toxins everywhere.

Zacchaeus

What was that wee little man Zacchaeus looking for when he climbed up into the sycamore tree? And why was he so anxious to see the One who was coming?

John the Baptizer is in the area of the Jordan warning whoever will listen, that the One everybody's been waiting for is on his way. This One will straighten things, he will make all things equal, even, and smooth - He's just around the corner. Get ready, you'd better be ready. Come and join the ones who are changing their ways in preparation. Large crowds of people journeyed down to the river to hear this prophet, and his convincing words made them ask, "Tell us what to do! How do we get ready?!"

This is it! I mean, for the Christian faith, this is it! It's here! This is the announcement of the imminent arrival of Jesus and all the work he will do. All of the next 2,000 years' worth of the Christian faith, (for good or bad) is set into motion on the heels of this announcement. And if I were to redact our Christian priorities back these 2,000 years and onto the lips of this guy, I would've expected him to say something like, "You need to attend synagogue more regularly, observe Torah more stringently, pray more, and with more fervor, give more to our Temple fund, etc." I mean, the religious condition of this peasantry who was harassed and oppressed on every side, (including by their religious leaders, especially by their religious leaders) couldn't have been in the best of shape. But he says nothing at all like that. What John tells the throngs of people is, "Whoever has two coats must share with anyone who has none, and whoever has food must do likewise." What?!! Jesus is coming. He's right around the corner. And what do we do to get ready? Share our stuff? (what little we have) That's it? You're not gonna give us anything more theologically challenging than that?

Nope.

Looks like the taxpayers got the day off too. When they asked what it was that they should do in order to get ready, (this was an easy one) John told them to stop collecting "more than the amount prescribed for you." In other words, stop contributing to the systems of oppression and injustice – no more extortion of the poor! He told the soldiers on watch, their partners in crime, essentially the same thing. Now it stands to reason that if the taxpayers got the afternoon off to hike down to the river, their supervisor would've taken the trip with them. And one of these guys would be Zacchaeus, our wee little man of the children's song. So back to the question. Why was this supervisor of tax collectors so eager to see this Jesus? Eager enough to climb a tree in anticipation?

The small band on the distant horizon that contained Jesus finally arrives. Jesus tells Zacchaeus to come down, he wants to come in, presumably to rest up and have a word. Maybe to ask him how this extortion thing's goin' cause Luke tells us that "Zacchaeus stood there and said to the Lord, 'Look, half of my possessions, Lord, I will give to the poor; and if I have defrauded anyone of anything, I will pay back four times as much.'"

I think Zacchaeus was anxious to see Jesus because he had heard John and had changed his ways. He was eager to answer that question in the affirmative, and anyone who could prove otherwise would collect four times the amount taken. I'd like to think that the supervisor's change in ways had a ripple effect across those who reported to him. I think I'm hoping for too much.

This story is profoundly telling. Because 2,000 years later, the theological complexities and institutional sophistication of the Christian faith and its influence across the world, and particularly in legislative halls across our country, has all but drowned out this simple message that is sung from the hearts of children. This man who exemplified the good news that Jesus was bringing with him, that these acts of mercy and the pursuit of justice would change the world, has become nothing more than a silly character in a nursery rhyme.

Children grow up and lose interest in climbing trees.

Patch Died That Night

A flash of spring weather and everyone's out of the house. For most of us, whether it's recreation or work, warmth makes everything more enjoyable. For those whose home *is* the outdoors, the warmth can actually be the difference between life and death. It is the light at the end of a cold dark tunnel mercifully coming into view. But not everyone makes it through to the other side. Regardless of what we believe through what is implied or explicitly claimed, or what most of us would understandably assume, there are nights well below freezing when some of the homeless among us are not welcomed inside *anywhere*. If we as a community don't know this, we do now.

January 8th was one such night. The low would be 26 degrees, and while most of us were turning the dial on our thermostats, "Patch," left with no other options, was helped out of his wheelchair by friends and put to bed on the hardened mud of an unsheltered camp. This hideously undignified piece of earth will forever mark the place where the candle of his life was permanently extinguished. Patch died that night and two days later would be unceremoniously buried in a muddy grave holding three inches of water. Though no less palatable, a passage from life to death like this might make sense on a remote battlefield, somewhere back in time, but not here and now – not in the center of this city. And yet it did. The night carried on – traffic crisscrossing overhead, theatres, restaurants, and bars letting out, a few dedicated runners passing by, night shifts getting into second gear, and University students preparing for the first days of school – all in the same city where a man lies dying of exposure to the cold.

However disturbing this is, the inexcusable and tragic insensitivities don't end with Patch's death. For reasons still unclear, the cause of Patch's death was attributed to his having a seizure, even though no autopsy was performed. Patch's sister, in her efforts to bring closure to her grief, made numerous attempts to offer documents verifying that Patch did not suffer from seizures, but the coroner's office would not return her repeated calls. It really is difficult to draw any other conclusion than one where the life and death of a homeless person is inconsequential and honoring his share in our common humanity and comforting his family is not worth the time or effort. In addition to these bitter frustrations, his sister is now left in a battle with insurance providers who do not want to honor covering the cost of Patches funeral because of the cause of death – an alleged seizure.

Patch deserves to be memorialized by those of us who knew him as being well-loved among his friends – a good man who laughed often. But what kind of a man Patch was is also inconsequential in light of this injustice. A human being's value and right to life and in particular, shelter from the elements, is not determined by their character, but by the intrinsic worth of their being alive. And this life can be raw, excruciatingly painful, and undignified for those who are caught in the grips of homelessness, but the answer is not found in some merciful relief in death. That sentiment is surely intended to assuage the conscience of those of us left alive.

Patches life is over. The warmth of the spring will never greet him again. But his story, the events that led to his death, the work to find justice and closure, and the fight to end death by homelessness is far from over.

Guilty

"He's gonna take the police officer's word over yours nine times out of ten."

Patrick returned to the courtroom pew where I was sitting and informed me that he'd be changing his plea from 'not guilty' to 'no contest' upon the advice of the bailiff. "But you're not guilty!" I said, the volume of my voice not really qualifying as a whisper anymore. "I know. But what can I do? He's right."

Patrick was in the city center one evening engaged in his work with the street paper when someone came up and took a seat beside him. This individual had been drinking and wasn't yet done. That's when the officer came up, took Patrick's new bench neighbor away for public intoxication, and issued Patrick a citation for violating the open container ordinance. I had come along to court with Patrick in support and to vouch for his character. I've known Patrick for over a year and have never seen him intoxicated. Patrick enjoys a drink the same as many of the rest of us do, but doesn't drink in public – ever, unlike many of the rest of us do. We knew it was going to be his word against the officer's and though we weren't suggesting that there was a sinister motive behind the issuance of the citation, we were suggesting that anyone can make a mistake – even a police officer. And in this case, according to Patrick, he had.

As Patrick looked at me, waiting for approval, I realized just how easy it is for me to slip into an ideal world where we could have actually reasoned with blind justice that a homeless man's word was just as credible as a police officer's *and* that a homeless man could muster up the resolve to assert so. Patrick, however, was fully willing to accept the thirty-day probation, pay the court costs, and resume his place in society – complete with the readiness to be drug back in before the judge if and when he should ever inadvertently find himself near an open container of alcohol, and an officer of the law should decide again to act on the tired assumption that if you're homeless, you're drinking.

There are some ideals that are more difficult to see realized than others. For example, ideally, my favorite restaurant would relocate across the street from my office rather than further down the avenue. But that's not gonna happen and there's nothing I can do about it. Ideally, the car with the "Choose Life" license plate would not carelessly run me off the road, but all my swearing won't change that either, (and ideally, I wouldn't be swearing). However, there are some ideals that we can attain to by simply choosing to attain to them. Particularly how we choose to value one another outside the stereotypes we construct. Our stereotypes crystallize how we function, or even if we can function within our societies. This is an example of how something gets created out of nothing – stereotypes create a real-world order from perceived assumptions. Assumptions that don't exist outside our minds. The end results are generally the same and are always more taxing on the underprivileged and marginalized. Patrick is ready to plead "guilty" or "no contest" even though he's innocent. But he also knows there's an order that he is powerless to overcome and though he doesn't accept the charge, he accepts the punishment and the cost and contributes to the reinforcement of someone else's truth and order.

A truth and order that is based on the assumptions that nine times out of ten, a police officer is trustworthy, and a homeless man is not.

It's Like They Found a Talking Dog

I Am Malala, is the inspirational autobiography of a young Pakistani girl who refused to be silenced by the Taliban while fighting for her rights to an education – a fight that resulted in a gunshot to her head while on a bus ride home from school and which nearly cost this young girl her life. I remember being absolutely starstruck when the story broke back in 2012 and Malala Yousafzai was making her interview rounds. This is the kind of person that I want my daughter to be inspired by, and was so pleased to see that she was currently reading the book. Because of the persistence of Islamophobia here in the States, I thought to myself that this would be a great book to add to required reading lists for our schools, particularly our high schools. I asked my daughter how she was enjoying the book, and she replied that she had just started it and was needing some help on understanding who exactly is the Taliban. So I did the best I could, but then suggested she ask one of her best friends who is actually Muslim, she would surely be able to give a better explanation than I could.

We have known the family of this friend for seven or eight years – the entire time we've been in this city, and so I was confused when I heard that her answer came back accompanied with her father's opinion that he thought the book should be banned! This is such a wonderful story! This is such a wonderful young person! I thought that this is exactly what the doctor ordered for American Muslim families who have to live under the constant stigma and scrutiny that comes with uninformed stereotypes. Knowing that the vast majority of this population of Americans awake every day to the automatic and unfounded assumptions that characterize them based on the behavior of a few, I couldn't understand how the story of this young heroic Muslim could be anything short of their star witness. But that, I was to find out, was *exactly* the issue.

The inspiration of the story is not simply that Malala is of the Muslim faith, it is that she is a member of the human race, and a fairly new one at that. She could have been anything else, she could have been a boy, she could have been sixty years old and living in Iceland. She could have been standing against any one of this world's injustices and could have been a person of any faith or no faith and the story would still be inspiring. But what can happen when one assigns stardom to her based upon her faith, is that you identify her as an exception to the rule and thereby unknowingly and unintentionally reinforce the stigma. You can be misunderstood as saying, "this is a rare one" and therefore she is to be honored for exceptional behavior – not exceptional behavior in the sense that it's rare for humans to exhibit this level of courage, (especially children) but in the sense that it's rare for someone of the Muslim faith to exhibit such goodness, and it is in fact her courage as a human being that is exceptional, not her being a good person in spite of being Muslim.

If you're a person of the Muslim faith, the last thing you need perpetuated is some insulting notion that Malala is exceptional because she is a person of strong character *and believe it or not*, she's Muslim. In my opinion, banning the book may be a bit too strong a reaction, however when I look at it through the lens of communities that I belong to, maybe not. One's reaction to an issue, when seen from the perspective of an "insider" is usually very different from those looking at it from the outside, regardless of how sympathetic or supportive they may be.

Maybe if I'm an American Muslim, I just don't want to hear the word "Taliban" regardless of why or how it's being used, even in the context of a heroic young girl fighting against it. Maybe I just want it all to go away so that I can just be an American, not an American with an asterisk that says, "this one's not part of the Taliban."

Consider those who run for public office. How many are running on the assurance that they are actually honest? All the way back to and before "Honest Abe Lincoln." Not that most politicians are dishonest, they're not, but there is a real need to fight against the perceptions that they are. Again, the insider perspective is working overtime, unlike congress (see?) to separate the influence that the few behavioral issues can have on the rest. To those of us outside these groups or communities, it's easy to miss how sensitive those inside become to even the slightest reinforcements of damning stereotypes.

In February of 2013, a woman in Kansas City was giving some of her spare change to a homeless man whom she passed on the street nearly every day. This day, however, she not only gave him some spare change but accidentally dropped her $4000.00 engagement ring into his cup. Assuming she'd never see it again, she approached the man the next day, squatted down, and asked, 'Do you remember me?'

The man replied, 'I don't know. I see a lot of faces.'
'I might have given you something very valuable.'
'Was it a ring?'
'Yeah.'
'Well, I have it.'

As the woman tells the story, she said that 'It seemed like a miracle!' I remember when this story came out and it was making headlines all over the country. I also remember asking one of my homeless friends what he thought of the story. "I hate it!" he said. "It sends the message that we're all crooks except this guy. It's like, 'Hey everyone! Look over here, I've found an honest homeless man! This belongs in the newspaper!' It's like they found a talking dog or something"

Now, of course, not everyone is going to share the opinions of these people. I'm sure there are those out there who would say, "Hey, I'll take all the good press I can get!" Even those of us who work among the homeless community, and particularly in advocacy, are tempted to trumpet these kinds of stories because, on the one hand, they do help to undermine the assumption that as my friend said, the homeless are "all crooks." But on the other hand, they can send an unintended message that this man is an exception to the rule and that this is what makes this man such a hero and his story newsworthy – newsworthy to outlets all across the country! This man, Billy Ray Harris, is exceptional for a number of reasons, but maybe the fact that he passed up a free $4,000.00 that many of the rest of us might not have is what's newsworthy, regardless of his housing status.

Much like the inspirational courage of a young girl to fight injustice, regardless of what faith she belongs to.

I Need You to Pray for Me

I'm sitting in the office, frustrated over my lack of ability to focus on finishing this work that is long past due when I hear my assistant's voice outside the door asking, "Can I help you? Pastor Eddie is not available right now." With confidence that she will care for our visitor, I try gathering my thoughts again only to be distracted by a familiar voice, "No, this is a spiritual matter. I need to speak with Pastor Eddie." I rise from my chair, open the door, and welcome my long-time friend Gary (perhaps as chronically homeless a person as there is in this city) in for a visit. Gary sits down, scans the wreckage on my desk (and I think from his expression, he genuinely feels more pity for me than I do him), shakes his head, looks up at me, and says, "I need you to pray for me." And this is when a new level of frustration sets in.

Of course, I'm pleased to pray with Gary, that's not my frustration. And as I was a person of faith, I never underestimated the power and pleasures of a God. My frustration is with how often times we knowingly or unknowingly perpetuate the idea that homelessness can simply be prayed away. And this is exactly what Gary wants me to do for him. We do a great disservice to Gary, others experiencing homelessness, and ourselves if we treat prayer like Aladdin's lamp. I try and understand the posture Gary has assumed – the distrust of and the abandonment by a world that is meant to sustain him but instead vacillates from ignoring him to harassing him, sometimes all within the span of an hour. The predictable consequence is for one like Gary to seek help beyond the world that has betrayed him. He doesn't really want to wait for heaven, there's a sense that this life should matter now. The tragic irony is that those who are praying for God's will to be realized "here on earth as it is in heaven" are sometimes the ones confirming Gary's suspicion that ever realizing this heaven on earth is a lost cause. Those taught to pray this prayer are also the ones who are told to then go and do something about it.

Each of us possesses varying powers of reason, creativity, resourcefulness, and compassion – all the tools necessary, (and if you're a person of faith, God-given tools) to resolve this epidemic of disenfranchisement and homelessness. And when we unite these tools in a community-orchestrated effort, the power grows and becomes exponentially more effective. I know that there are legions of good people in this community who pray daily for the mass of oppressed humanity that smolders in the pit of the "mission district." I'm one of them. But what would it look like for a community to then rise up off its knees and intentionally pursue the work of reshaping the structures of society in such a way that even the modest dreams of having a place to call home and a sense of belonging can be realized by everyone?

What if our communities and their leaders were as diligent in these efforts as we are in pursuing the perpetual prosperity of those of us living and working in the mainstream? Can those who pray be honest enough to admit that maybe it's just easier for us to try and pray this dilemma away rather than rolling up our sleeves and applying ourselves to the task? There's a comforting strategy that gets applied instead to situations where there is a gap in our understanding and/or our level of commitment to work at a problem, and that is we stick God in there to bridge that gap. Our community's homelessness epidemics are complex and will require a substantial commitment if they are to be eliminated and are therefore fertile grounds for such a strategy. However, I am convinced that bridging that gap must include our community's willingness to act.

It's not that I want Gary, (or our community) to stop praying.

I just look forward to the day when Gary's prayers will be prayers of thanksgiving, for living in a community that is committed to the principle that everyone who desires a home should have a home.

Lost Sheep

The Homeless Collective has been holding weekly meetings at a local Ministry's "Outreach Service" for nearly two years. The event takes place every Wednesday night under the overpass that acts as a partial ceiling to the Mission District. Anywhere from 150-250 people sit at rows and rows of metal folding tables where they are served a meal, or stand in lines for clothing and blankets, or are directed to trailers where periodic medical and dental assistance is offered, all to the backdrop of a Christian church service. There is a "prayer table" and most nights an altar call stirring to repentance those for whom I presume are the "lost sheep" and needing to be found, a reference to one of Jesus' parables. In this parable, the lost sheep is a sinner in need of repentance and bringing back into the fold. It's difficult to stomach the arrogance of this organization's sentiment toward the poor it serves – transparently evident in its very name. But it is unapologetically thick with this Christian message and intentions directed towards these ones who are predominately from the homeless community.

Because it's a scheduled event that the Collective members regularly attend, it's been convenient for them to meet on these nights and with the large number of people from the homeless community who also attend, it's been one of our best recruitment opportunities. Every table is involved in some conversation, ours just happens to be our work at hand. We've never been a distraction nor have we undermined the event or the organization that runs it, regardless of our opinions of it, but on this night our table conversation was interrupted by the very unnerved and angry operations manager. Looking at me and my coworkers, "Y'all need to come with me right now! Right now! I need to talk to you behind the trailer.. right now!" We left the table and followed. After being interrogated about our political intentions, and having one of my colleagues threatened with the cops removing her, we agreed to respect their organization's space and leave.

My appeals to their Christian bible fell on deaf ears. The prophet sums up all of what is required of humans in Micah 6.8, and that is "to do justice and love kindness (or mercy)." It's no surprise that the Christian communities have excelled in loving mercy, even if not for the purest of reasons, but have failed miserably when it comes to doing justice. The pursuit of justice costs far more than blankets and food, it requires us to call out and change the systems that create and perpetuate the need to hand out blankets and food. I explained to the operations manager that our works of justice should be seen by them as complementing their works of mercy in completing this holy directive. I argued in vain that justice is achieved in the political realm as the terror in his countenance only confirmed my wasted breath. It's easy to conclude that organizations like this fear the threat of making redundant the mercy industry, but what's probably closer to the truth is their fear of the threat to the political machines that they support and who reinforce their posture – that the poor are sinners and they have no one to blame but themselves for their being marginalized outside "the flock."

The Homeless Collective will continue its work, and our objective is to ultimately put organizations like this one out of business. But shouldn't that be their objective as well?

Shouldn't we all be working towards just communities that no longer require people to depend upon the mercy of others to survive?

The Shelter of Last Resort

Cities across the country are pursuing aggressive policies aimed at the homeless, but the executive director of the National Law Center on Homelessness and Poverty, characterized Columbia, South Carolina's *"Columbia Cares"* initiative to be "an extreme, highly disturbing example." And she's right.

This past month, Columbia's City Council unanimously approved a plan that would essentially make it illegal to be homeless in Columbia, particularly in the metropolitan area where the city is striving for economic revival and the Mayor asserts that "We've got to make sure that every single thing we do focuses on continuing to attract advancement... Nothing can be a distraction." The plan's architect, a council member, regards the homeless and their presence in the city as, "...a giant risk to business." In reading through the *Columbia Cares* plan, I don't recall if it ever sited exactly what Columbia *cares* about. It certainly cannot be referencing their care for the homeless.

The plan does begin with a dose of reason: the proposal of an induction center that would become the "front door" through which one's needs are identified and can then be directed to the applicable community resources. However, the plan loses all sense of reasoning soon after that and becomes scary instead. The plan states that if the homeless violate existing laws such as loitering, panhandling, or urban camping – laws that blatantly target the homeless, they must go to the induction center, go to jail or leave town. Both the police and "every neighbor" can call and have someone in violation of these picked up and either recycled through this induction center or go to jail. The induction center, by the way, is not a shelter. I'm not sure where one goes after the induction center, but in *Columbia Cares'* plan there is no emergency shelter, only The Retreat, "the shelter of last resort" located 10 to 15 miles outside the downtown area. The Retreat is a proposed 100 plus acre privately owned facility that will house those who are found mentally or physically deficient. Out of sight and out of mind from the rest of civil society.

If you look at the councilman's page on The City of Columbia's website, you'll find the claim that "his model for elected leadership is the 19th century statesman William Wilberforce." Now, most of us know Wilberforce for his work in the abolition of the slave trade in Britain, but many of us also know that Wilberforce supported the abolition of *habeas corpus* – the principle that ensures a prisoner can be released from unlawful detention—that is, detention lacking sufficient cause or evidence. And when it comes to Wilberforce's theological views on the poor, he supported "the rich man in his castle, the poor man at his gate" as the natural order of things and preached to the poor that: *"their more lowly path has been allotted to them by the hand of God; that it is their part faithfully to discharge its duties and contentedly to bear its inconveniences..."* I'm not sure how vibrant the city of Columbia's slave trade is, so I might be more easily convinced that by claiming Wilberforce as a model, this councilman means to communicate his posture on the natural place of the poor among us – 15 miles away from the rich man's castle and perhaps his feelings on the basic human rights of those relegated to jails or maybe even worse – The Retreat.

How will The Retreat be funded? At least in part by those who will be "retreating" there. This facility and other programs will be defrayed in part by "payments currently being lost" such as food stamps, housing, and disability. In other words, it sounds as though your social security check will be signed over to the staff. This is appalling, especially in light of the fact that many of those sent to The Retreat will be members of the community whose mental or physical un-wellness will cause them to be there.

There's more to this disturbing plan than what can be covered here. We will be following it closely, not least of all because Columbia is not far from us, and we could potentially find ourselves welcoming their exiles. We would also hate to see other cities look to *Columbia Cares* as a pattern on how to criminalize homelessness.

Columbia Cares is both an insult to the homeless of Columbia and a shameful deception in its name, which implies its motives are driven by a compassionate posture towards those they are simultaneously criminalizing. Unless of course, we are meant to understand that Columbia in fact cares about the rich men and their castles.

Then it makes perfect sense.

When I Get Home

"I'm gonna tell God all my troubles, When I get home...
I'm gonna tell him the road was rocky When I get home."
"We'll soon be free, When de Lord will call us home.
My brudder, how long, 'Fore we done sufferin' here,
It won't be long
'Fore de Lord will call us home..."

Like these, many of the spiritual songs of the early American slaves pointed to their longing to go "home." And of course, home is heaven – the afterlife. The sense that this world is not my home was born more out of their experience of pain and suffering than any theological conclusions reached from Bible study. People of faith orientate their posture on life based on their holy writ; however, there are times when their experience is so strong, so overwhelming, that they are compelled to reconcile Scripture with their life experience – their beliefs must correspond with their perceived realty, or the basis and foundation of their faith is shaken. So the idea that this life, here and now, should be experienced at its fullest and richest is missed because there is no apparent hope, no way of conceiving of this life flourishing with purpose and meaning. These ideas were not unique to this generation of sufferers, nor did they originate with them, but it does illustrate well how the hopes and dreams of the oppressed are transferred from this life onto the next.

But it's a long time until heaven.

So how do we cope in a world that doesn't feel like home? Home is a place (with lamentable exceptions) of belonging, a place where things are right, a place where one's pursuit of happiness is supported, celebrated, and defended. For so many of us, we have some connectivity, some familiarity with the intended flourishing of the goodness of life. But if we're honest, it's not complete. Most of us carry the sense that in many ways, things are just not right. That's why we ask questions like, "What's wrong?" We have almost a universal standard by which we judge our human experience, and we only seem to be able to capture from time to time the glimpses of its measuring up. There is a constant struggle to reach that plateau where life levels off and aberrations like pain and sadness are gone. Whether you believe it exists or not, we really do long for a heaven – a time and place of wholeness and wellness of life – a restoration and mending of the constantly unraveling fabric of this world. A place called home.

But we know that things matter now. We are here now. We know that there is a richness to this life that transcends the temptation to believe that this is nothing more than an entrance exam. And that is what can drive the poor and oppressed to despair. It's a misinformed conclusion to suggest that alcohol and substance abuse among the homeless is the cause any more than it is the effect. There is a wholeness and wellness that many of us believe will be, ought to be sought after, and cultivated here and now. And very few are ever truly consoled with the promise of "pie in the sky," the prescription given to the poor by the privileged that, "Your life is hard now, and that's none of my concern, but do what's right and you'll eat pie like me when this life is over."

Acknowledging that we cannot create a heaven on earth does not prevent us from searching for and embracing whatever goodness is out there for us to find and to share. Our hope for the future does not need to disregard the present any more than the meaning we find in the present satisfies any sense that there is a completeness yet to come. Becoming cultivators of wholeness and wellness can both figuratively and literally provide the homes that we all long for, here and now.

The Needy

We *need* a new car,
We *need* a vacation,
We *need* it to stop raining,
We *need* to find a place to park!
And most of all... we *need* a new coach...

We are needy people. we use these or any number of similar exclamations, we don't really mean to convey that we are in a predicament that is so dire that we are to be pitied, (although the ease with which we throw the word around and the things we apply it to does in fact reveal something of the pitiful nature of how we most often see and judge the severity of our "first world" predicaments). But one who is to be pitied, or a pitiful person, is exactly the image that the term "needy" conjures up. It certainly isn't a compliment. It is a condescending label we attach to those living in poverty.

We are needy people.

Of course, the word "need" is a relative term. It assumes there is something contingent upon this thing we *need* to happen or this thing we *need* to get or have. There are times when we legitimately *need* a parking spot, or we really do *need* a vacation, (I'm not sure how often we really do *need* a new coach), but the legitimacy of the needs for those of us who live well above the poverty level lies in the fact that some degree of happiness is at stake.

We *need* this new app,
We *need* more friends (or less),
We *need* a refill at the restaurant,
We *need* to be left alone...
But most often, our survival, our very existence does not depend upon the things we say we need.

We are needy people.

I think we'd be shocked, or amused, by the number of times during the course of a day we started a sentence with, "I need to..." or, "you need to..." or ended it with, "... that's just what I needed." But as often as we use the word, we still would not consider ourselves "needy" and would probably be offended by someone referring to us as "needy." Even those of us who have had or do need life-preserving assistance would not want to be labeled as "the needy." We have needs, but we're not "needy."

We are all needy people.

I cringe when I hear someone refer to "the needy", and although I'm sure that most times the speaker doesn't mean anything derogatory by it, it is still a condescending label that they wouldn't want to be turned back on them. The number of needs among those living at or below the poverty level is certainly no more than those of us living above it. But the label "*the* needy" is reserved for those who exist in a state of poverty – a state of being in need of the things in life to actually preserve their lives, and not a certain state of happiness. (And I would contend that there is an unflattering reference to one's character attached). The irony is that typically the more we have, the more we tend to need or think we need. If I didn't have the privilege of owning a car, I wouldn't need a parking space; if I didn't have the privilege of work, I wouldn't need a vacation; if I didn't have the privilege of eating out, I wouldn't need my server to refill my drink...

So, who really are "the needy"?

If measured by the frequency of our own words, we are all an absolutely needy bunch.

...who really need to stop using the label "needy"

Home-Grown Refugees

Early morning of December 17th. My coworker and I were treated to a sampling of the city's assortment of tired rhetoric intended to defend the eviction of the homeless community from under the I-40 overpass. It began with the humanitarian clean up pitch (which is negated by the 'inhumanitarian' eviction), moved to the presence of criminal activity, (I should expect that the next time someone in my suburban neighborhood is involved in criminal activity, the bulldozers are on their way), and naturally on to the concerns of the surrounding businesses (I was actually embarrassed for him as his hand gesture invited me to survey the surrounding businesses he was referring to – it's a fucking overpass!).

These are obvious smokescreens, but then to launch into the claim that the city uses these evictions as "an opportunity to route people to good services" is a self-inflicted insult, revealing their complete ignorance, or their desperate hopes in the ignorance of the listener. But of course, this isn't happening, no one's being 'routed' anywhere. They're being scattered and told to find places that are out of public view. And so at least the sting of the insult that this claim would have on these home-made refugees isn't added to the injury of their dragging their belongings to who knows where. No one is being 'routed' to any magical services that are going to whisk them out from underneath the bridges and into the comfort of their own home the next day. This is as nonsensical as the groups who are trying to pray people off the streets. The effectiveness of these services and their ability to come to bear on the varied lives of the homeless are exceedingly complex. And most of the people who are living in the woods and under the bridges represent the problems for whom these services have no easy answers to. And if the city actually believes in the strategy of this 'opportunity' then it assumes that the homeless have to be nearly forced into accessing these services, which in turn assumes that homelessness is the result of people willingly refusing these resources, and so then the solution to homelessness is to harass them to the point that they will finally come to their senses and turn loose of this idyllic life of pain and despair. Following this logic, we could have saved a lot of time, energy, and resources by crafting a plan to address homelessness in our city with just the one strategy of whipping and herding these people into housing.

Afterward, we sat together on one of the coldest mornings of this season, huddled around the warmth of a fire produced by one piece of wood. The low for the night before was 28 degrees and this day would only see a windy high of 44. It was a week before Christmas and in came the refugees, carrying and dragging their homes and belongings – the homeless campers who had just a couple of hours earlier been evicted by the city. Their faces were truly pitiful – tired, cold, scared, and miserable as they were welcomed with open arms to squeeze into an already overcrowded homeless community. Moments later, the police come into the camp and with a glow of satisfaction, the officer announces that *their* eviction notice would be coming in about a week and proceeds to check I.D.s and take everyone's names. If so, that would be Christmas Eve. Those of us who had come out to meet with the Homeless Collective sat speechless – disgusted and ashamed of our city.

The following day, in an inauguration speech, our mayor spoke about what they believe makes a city great, including a willingness to open its arms...

*"We know that a great city opens its arms to celebrate and nurture the diversity of its people- from white-collar to blue-collar; from labor to management; from every neighborhood north, south, east, west, and downtown; people of all races and colors; people of all abilities; gay and straight; people of all faiths; from the youngest to the oldest; from the richest to **the poorest.**"*

I don't know... I think the greatness of a city is measured much like the greatness of a person, by how it treats those who have little or nothing to contribute to its greatness.

But even by the mayor's standards, this city missed the mark of greatness on the morning they were probably polishing this speech.

Nervous, and Speaking
in Guarded Tones

For years, I'd heard stories about it. So on Thursday night, August 11, I decided to go undercover and see for myself what a night at our city's primary homeless shelter "mission" would be like.

I was coming in late, so I entered the front desk rather than the Welcome Center. I would need to do that the following morning. The process for a one-night temporary stay was incredibly easy, and the person who signed me in was kind and polite. Within five to ten minutes, I was given my temporary card and instructions for the night. I went back outside and across the street to talk with my friend Johnny. Johnny doesn't stay at the mission, he camps. But with his Homeless Management Information Service (HMIS) card, he can have a meal, a shower, and check his mail there.

Johnny and I walked in together and had dinner before going out the back to the small courtyard for a few cigarettes where he gave me the rundown of what I could expect and how to go about making sure I got a bottom bunk. They're preferable. We hung out in the courtyard for the next couple of hours and the night was looking fairly uneventful until it happened. I saw through the windows into the lobby area an altercation between a young woman and a security guard. It appeared that the girl was trying to pull away from the guard's grasp and several of the "guests" outside began to gather and watch.

After a few moments, the police came on the scene and began to escort the girl out the front door. It was nine o'clock and Johnny was heading in to get his shower. I couldn't imagine a scenario that would require the police, so I went in to ask around to see what had happened. No one seemed to want to talk about it. They were nervous and speaking in guarded tones. One "guest" however did tell me that the young woman was pregnant and didn't deserve to be thrown out to the streets. Another said that the girl had cursed at the staff. "This is a church; you can't do that. Would you cuss in a church?" he asked. I didn't say anything because he wouldn't have liked my answer. "Just keep to yourself and be polite to the staff, and you'll be alright," he assured me as he walked away. The person at the front desk called out for everyone to clear the lobby. At this point, my intended stay was over. I knew I had to go outside and check on the girl, and because the mission's doors are locked at six-thirty, I was not going to be allowed back in.

I walked out the front door to four police cars, lights flashing, and a group of officers huddled near the entrance. I looked around for terrorists in handcuffs, because I mean, surely to god an eighteen-year-old pregnant girl being asked to leave doesn't require this amount of force. But everything was still and quiet, except for the young girl sitting on the sidewalk, about twenty yards away, and crying.

I walked over, sat down beside the girl, and asked if I could help get her a room for the night. "All I wanted was to get my book, have a shower, and go to bed. I'm so tired," she said through her tears. We introduced ourselves to one another, and I asked if she felt like talking about what had happened. "Look, if someone gets in my face and yells at me, I'm gonna yell back! I'm doing the best I can do. I take my meds." She was tired and traumatized and her trying to explain how this had come about was difficult to understand, but it had something to do with her wanting to go upstairs to the women's dorm to get her book. The last thing she needed at this point was someone trying to pull details out of her, so I just listened the best I could.

The girl told me that at some point early on in the altercation, presumably while being escorted back downstairs, the mission guard threatened to pepper-spray her in the elevator. "Wait, he threatened to pepper spray you?" I asked. "Yes! And how dumb is that anyway? We're inches away from each other in an elevator. He's gonna get as much of that as I am!" Just then one of her friends came out and joined us. We introduced ourselves and I finally told them who I was and why I was there. The girl's friend responded, "Really? I'd love to talk to you about all of this! I've known her since we were both eleven years old. She did not deserve this, no one deserves this. They threw me out in the middle of December because I wouldn't talk. I just didn't feel like talking to anyone that night and they said that if I wasn't going to talk then they couldn't help me, and I needed to leave. And it was cold that night! It was so cold that I walked over to the bus station and destroyed a newsstand just so I could get arrested and have someplace warm to stay."

She turned and asked her friend if she was okay, if she'd been hurt at all. Looking at me, she said, "They wrestled her to the ground."

"What? They wrestled you to the ground?" I asked her.

"Yes, the mission officer cornered me in the chapel and wrestled me to the ground."

I sat there, head in hands and in disbelief.

Subject to Raid and Confiscation at Any Moment

I grow increasingly troubled at night when my head finally hits the pillow and I sink into a world of peace and comfort that for many of our friends, if they have ever known this comfort, is a distant memory and a world that they may never know again. I've backpacked these mountains for thirty years and have endured the cold and wet with the confidence that the comfort of my home was only a decision away. I cannot imagine, however, huddled in my camp, (and that does not constitute a scenic spot tucked into the rhododendron with the running stream for ambiance) with little or no proper gear, the anxiety of knowing that my position is illegal and subject to raid and confiscation at any moment and that this is the extent of whatever comfort I may expect to enjoy with no end in sight. I could on the other hand opt for the local shelter where peace and comfort are usually nothing more than the subject of ones interrupted prayers. Through the course of a busy day, the overnight conditions of the homeless only register for fleeting moments while other concerns push to the front. It's at night when their conditions come back for center stage. You try not to think about it, or at least for too long, but it's like the persistence of a child's thoughts on Christmas Eve – until your consciousness finally gives up, you're sentenced to dwell on it.

It's not only the faces that scroll through my mind's eye but the person behind the face. The voice that I may have heard that very day telling stories, pleading for some kind of break to come their way, sharing with confidence the plans they know God has for them or cursing the empty existence into which they were born. There is a world contained behind the eyes of each of us, and when we speak, we do much more than transfer information, we welcome one another into these worlds.

Understanding which leads to sympathy is best cultivated when we make the effort to enter someone's world – when we speak, and when we listen. However, there is an investment that we make when we enter each other's worlds. One actually has a share in that person's world, and you will in some way and to some degree have a share in that person's experiences, and unfortunately, that includes their pains, fears, and sadness. This will then, in turn, ignite a sense of urgency when faced with the tragedies that come their way. Imagine you're walking through the city center, and you notice up ahead that someone has fallen and there is a growing circle of concerned people. You would most likely join them in their concern and hope and trust that someone will take care of them, but you're not really going to involve yourself until you notice, as you come closer, that the person who's fallen is a dear friend. That's when you drop everything to personally make sure that something is being done to bring them out of the trouble, and as quickly as possible.

Of course, it's not possible for everyone to engage with the homeless of our community with such an intimacy of friendship, but this street paper does try to provide a venue for the homeless to speak, to share their experiences, and welcome you into their world. We don't expect nor do we necessarily desire for you to lose any sleep over the desperate conditions of our community's homeless, but if we can help facilitate a sense of urgency among our community to bring about systemic wholeness, a little loss of sleep will be well worth it.

Dialogue and Interaction

"Whether true or false, what is said about men often has as much influence on their lives, and particularly on their destinies, as what they do." Victor Hugo, Les Misérables.

This street paper is often mistaken for a 'jobs program.' I heard it again just recently from a police officer who was trying to make sense of who we are and what we are trying to accomplish. The thought was that we are mentoring the homeless back into the working sector of society by training them through a small-scale employment model. The truth is, most of our homeless friends do not need to be taught how to work – they just need the opportunity to work. This paper exists rather to deconstruct the myths and stigmas attached to the homeless that typically prevent them from gaining meaningful employment. This has worked for at least three of our solicitors who have landed jobs as a direct result of their work with us – not however because they have been trained how to work, but because of the willingness of a local employer to take the rare chance on hiring an individual experiencing homelessness because of that personal interaction. When we sign an individual up for the paper, we establish first and foremost that they are becoming an ambassador for their community – that they may earn some cash in the process, but the primary purpose is to engage with people of the mainstream that they would most likely, under any other circumstance never speak a word to. No matter how much ink I or any other contributor spills on the issues of homelessness, there is nothing more powerful or compelling than the human element of personal interaction across the boundaries of economic positions.

Of course, we try to make the economic experience of our solicitors as productive as possible, with our motives being geared towards creating incentives for them to develop greater connectivity with our efforts in moving them towards the stability of housing. This has happened with several of our solicitors, and it is very satisfying to hear some refer to themselves as "formerly homeless," but even as significant as this is, we still hope that greater opportunities may come for all those experiencing homelessness in our community through the human aspect of interaction combined with the information provided within the pages.

So to you our readers, as we approach our second year anniversary, we want you to know that not only have you provided for the rare dignity of ordering off of a menu, the comfort that comes from wearing freshly washed clothes, the occasional rest and solitude of a night's stay in a hotel room, transportation (other than walking), minutes on a phone, and a host of other minor expenditures that most of us take for granted, you have also helped us in opening up some much-needed dialogue between neighbors who are sometimes mutually suspicious of one another, and have assisted in at least 14 of our solicitors being able to refer to themselves as "formerly homeless."

We believe Victor Hugo was right – and that what's being said in and through this paper is having a positive influence on the destinies of those experiencing homelessness here in our community. We also believe that through continued dialogue and interaction, we may also change the destiny of our community itself.

We Can't Walk in Their Shoes

Irrespective of one's feelings about Christmas, its message this time of year is almost inescapable – even the air we breathe contains the sounds of its carols and it sets me thinking of the seemingly subtle yet significant difference between God walking among humanity and God entering into humanity. It is a message that fills our senses: we see it, smell it, taste it, and we may not believe it, but we hear it. Whether or not you believe the principle behind the message is divine, it is a principle that, at the least, wisdom tells us to apply to everything – you treat the cause, not just the symptoms.

Occasionally I read of someone who temporarily steps out of his or her life of relative comfort to purposefully experience homelessness. Usually, this is done with the noble intent of both gaining a personal appreciation for what those experiencing homelessness have to endure on a daily basis and raising public awareness of the issue itself. Just recently a pastor and his youth director in Norman, Oklahoma took a ten-day trip into homelessness for these two reasons. It takes courage to pull this off, and there are not many of us who would willingly invite the discomfort and danger of living on the streets into our lives, and their account speaks to this. They describe the difficulties of finding a place to sleep for the night, the unsettling glares from those in the community that they have entered as strangers, and although three meals a day were easy to come by, there was no mention of one of the often-overlooked aspects of homelessness – there's no such thing as asking, "What do you want for dinner tonight?" or a New Year's resolution to begin a nutritionally healthier diet – you get what you get.

But the simulation ends there. We can experience the bad food, the uncomfortable sleeping arrangements, the uncertainty and fear of the company around us, the lack of money, the frigid cold and unbearable heat, the lack of adequate clothing, and the constant fatigue- but the one thing we cannot simulate, nor experience is the hopelessness of life without a home. This is the aspect of homelessness that we cannot share through a temporary excursion nor soothe through our charities. We can't reverse someone out of homelessness with food and clothing any more than we can cure an illness with painkillers or rekindle a pilot light by heating up the radiators.

As noble and useful as these excursions among the homeless can be, they can also perpetuate the unfortunate conclusion that homelessness is the sum of the experience rather than the result of causes that although we may not be able to share, we can and must address. For example, too many families in East Tennessee have to choose between paying rent or buying food. More than

75% of low-income renter households spend more than 50% of their income on rent and utilities leaving less than 50% of their income for food, medicine, transportation, childcare, clothing, and other essential expenses. (source: National Low Income Housing Coalition, 2012). These are the households that are most vulnerable to becoming homeless, and they are increasing in number each day. Recovery from homelessness as a result of inadequate income and/or affordable housing can be extremely difficult. The circumstances that lead to one's inadequate income are not likely to be enhanced by your new address being the local mission- and are compounded daily by the deterioration of one's will and determination through the entanglement in hopelessness and despair. This cannot be simulated, but it is reality and represents one of the root causes of homelessness that must be addressed.

We assign our deepest feelings and our most profound thoughts to song. I hear the choral voices reach the crescendo *O night divine*, and am moved to reflect on the deep, deep significance that these words hold for those of the Christian faith – the night in which God entered the hopelessness of humanity through the birth of Jesus. Addressing our predicament at the root cause, and redeeming the hope for peace on earth and goodwill towards men.

Are You Going to Heaven?

"Again I tell you, it is easier for a camel to go through the eye of a needle than for someone who is rich to enter the kingdom of God." ~ Jesus of Nazareth.

For a person of the Christian faith, the words of Jesus are very difficult. Not because they're so hard to understand, but because they are so easily understood. And if you're of the Christian faith, you've claimed solidarity with Jesus and his worldview.

I remain convinced that the greatest hurdle one must clear in order to confront and potentially connect with the purity of Jesus is those of us who wear his name. I'm reminded of the interview with Eric Idle of Monty Python some years ago. In the interview, he was asked to defend the controversial film, *The Life of Brian,* as to many Christians it seemed to be making fun of Jesus. Idle's response was that it was in fact their intent in the beginning, but after preparing for the film by reading through the life and sayings of Jesus, they couldn't find anything to ridicule, but that the profundity of his words only brought into greater contrast the lives of those who claim to follow him. This is what the film then pursued – his disciple's almost seemingly intentional complicating of something so simple in order to avoid following it.

There have been drums of ink spilled over the text above – mostly not in order to make it understandable, but to make it *followable*. I think the driving formula runs something like this: *bad people don't go to heaven, riches make people bad, and therefore rich people don't go to heaven.* But riches don't make people bad, and Jesus wasn't referring to heaven. *The kingdom of God* to many is an antiquated term that few in the western world can access a point of reference to make any sense of. *The kingdom of God* is simply the realm in which one find's his peace, love, and justice steering the course of renewal among both this world and our relationships, and this most certainly includes economic justice as is contained in Jesus' mission statement, "...to bring good news to the poor..." As Jim Wallis has said, "A gospel, (good news) that doesn't change the world only works for those who don't need the world changed." Jesus was perfectly capable of using hyperbole and the point he wants to make in the opening text is not that rich people are bad and an inheritance in the afterlife is impossible, but that it's difficult for any of us to surrender our wealth in order to bring about economic equality for the common good.

A pursuit of the common good, however, is exactly the posture one will assume when the kingdom of God finds fertile ground as is demonstrated by those recorded in *The Acts of The Apostles* who sought to establish such a community, going as far as liquidating their wealth in order to ensure adequate provisions for all, (something the *rich young ruler* was not able to do). I sometimes wonder how many of us western Christians could have made it past the first year or two of our faith if this was what it meant to enter and engage in the kingdom of God.

It's not easy to fight for systemic changes that can bring about economic justice, it comes much more naturally to fight for the things we have and the positions we've acquired while letting the disenfranchised fend for themselves – believing that our systems really do work equally well for everyone. Acknowledging the rightness of turning about-face and swimming against the long-entrenched stream of advantage is understandably a process. However, it is not impossible. Just difficult.

Spiral Of Violence

Late Tuesday night, April 9th, the Police responded to a disturbance just North of downtown, resulting in the investigation of a sprawl of campsites along the stream behind the abandoned buildings. Inside one of the tents lay the body of the first of three victims that would be discovered – all allegedly linked to the work of three homeless persons sleeping in the same tent. The homeless killing the homeless is particularly unnerving.

The accounts from the homeless community of what happened and why may be widely varied, but mainstream public response to these killings is far more singular and predicable – varying only in intensity. As an advocate for the homeless, my first response is a desire to put the public at ease so that the homeless may escape the typical reprisals of sweeping camps and profiling them out of our neighborhoods – to argue that the potential for violence runs through the hearts of all people, regardless of their housing status, and that being homeless does not make one any more susceptible to certain behaviors. But that's just not altogether true. It is true that we are all human and have the potential for some degree of violence, but we are fooling ourselves if we don't acknowledge that circumstances of radical poverty and disenfranchisement do not come to bear on one's behavior. And though it does not make one's behavior acceptable, it can make it explainable. This was a tragic event and there's no way to justify or legitimize it, but it would also be tragic in the long term for us to console ourselves by believing that the consequences of our systems of oppression are no more than the absence of the good life for the unfortunate ones who cannot attain to it. You simply cannot have a sub-class of humans living in sub-human conditions and be free from its consequences, and we know this. I've never seen a headline that reads, *"Housed man arrested for..."* The genesis of this repulsive act, whether greed, anger, hate, fear, or other, translates across the economic classes and there's no evidence to assert that these killings can be attributed to the simple fact the alleged were homeless. But how much of our prejudices against the homeless have to do with our expectations of them based on assumptions regarding pure human nature, and knowing how life on a sub-human level would affect those of us living above it? It is in fact remarkable that our communities don't experience more unrest from our homeless than they do.

Helder Camara, Archbishop of Olinda in the underdeveloped North-East Brazil in 1971, spoke of the "spiral of violence." He refers to the three acts of violence – the systemic oppression of the poor, the revolt of the poor, and the response to revolt through repression and restoring order. Camara speaks in particular about how this spiral of violence is played out in the global community, but I suggest this is at work on local and even personal levels as well. I would attribute to our extravagant systems of aid to the poor and homeless as the reason we are not seeing signs of a concerted revolt in our local communities. And it is this aid that forestalls the spiral, but for how long? The increased systemic violence against the poor and homeless is becoming more than what those involved in providing aid can overcome. When a mother of three is stretched beyond what she can manage on poverty-level income combined with over-priced housing and hair-trigger eviction notices, those of us who try and provide aid are at a loss. The collateral damage by one single misstep can literally extinguish one's future. When a young man faces a life of complete disenfranchisement because he is labeled a felon, a label that excludes him from our most basic community act of voting, severely restricts his opportunities to engage in the community's workforce and consequently live among us in inadequate housing, and then excludes him from much of the government aid intended to help clear hurdles like these, we create a marginalized individual loosely dwelling among us but not a part of the community and with little invested interests in adhering to the behavioral standards we set. And then we scratch our heads as to why. Almost daily he sees or reads of people in position and power who glide unharmed over similar or even more unlawful missteps and these dynamics fuel anxiety, fear, anger, and the potential abandonment of any desire or obligation to play by the rules this system, perceived as grossly unjust, has set. And once again, those of us on the private level of providing aid are at a loss.

All interactions have changed. There is no one set way in which the person experiencing this degree of poverty and homelessness responds to those sharing in their poverty or the others beyond it, but there's no doubt that it does affect the way someone sees him or herself and the world around them. To those living beyond the life of poverty, the interaction and relationship easily become one of condescension, whether intentional or not. It becomes a relationship of suzerainty where one acknowledges the position and power of the other and behaves accordingly. Those of us who work in the realm of distributing aid and/or fostering empowerment experience this all too often – presentations of worthiness can characterize even our most informal interactions and if we are not aware, we can reinforce an existing posture of a lack of self-worth or participate in the transference of it without ever knowing. Outside the pursuance of a genuine relationship among those we work with, we may also be unaware of the "masks" that are often employed in order to barter for aid when one has no tangible "thing" or achievement to satisfy. And we in the positions of privilege no doubt, whether intentionally or unintentionally, apply the pressure to resort to this behavior. John W. Blasingame argues in his *The Slave Community: Plantation Life in the Antebellum South* that the docile and childlike Sambo stereotype assigned to slaves was in fact a mask, a role that the slaves performed for their masters' edification which also served as a defense mechanism, allowing them to cope with the oppression of bondage. Those living in radical poverty who are not engaged in relationships outside their sub-community, and in particular, with no real connections with those who are able to provide aid, may have no reasons for demonstrating their worth or wearing this mask, and may also fall into a position of assuming that those in the mainstream are uninterested in their behavior or edification thereof, unless and until it affects them.

And so there is then the potential for those living in poverty to assign to one another the lack of intrinsic value or worth that they have reluctantly adopted from these unequal relationships. This is not at all unlike the great worth assigned among those of power to one another based on the other side of these same relationships, regardless of any objective deservedness. If you, like me, have no real value as a person because of your disconnectedness with the mainstream community (often translated, as "you're not being a *productive* member") then there is the potential for your surmising that whatever damage comes upon you is imperceptible and inconsequential. I say there is the potential because what we find to be overwhelmingly true is just the opposite, and that is why the alleged violence of the homeless killing the homeless is particularly unnerving to me. I believe it is in our nature to perceive and to have an inner sense, even against all foes, of our intrinsic worth as humans, and the unity and bond that is typically exemplified among the poor and homeless in struggling against all that seem to want to combat that is inspiring in ways that are difficult to put to words. The possibility that there exist those who have embraced this sub-human existence assigned it to their peers and assume the liberty to behave accordingly reveals a breakdown of this unity and the sad prospects of the potential loss of a common front. And the turning on one another is often the signs of a farewell to the hopes that things will ever change.

Rest In Peace

On April 9th our local paper reported the discovery of a body found underneath a downtown overpass. I read the account that morning and immediately knew that it was one of our neighborhood friends who live outside in the open spaces. Throughout the day I took note of who I had not seen while wondering who it was that I would never see again. These days are always the hardest. That night I laid awake thinking of this person living and dying outside the relational structures of our community, seeking their last place of shelter in and underneath the concrete structures of our community. My last thoughts were filled with wondering did they have last thoughts. As the sound of the traffic rushed overhead, did they know that the thoughts they were having were to be their last, or if they did, what were they? Unanswered prayers with promises made? Or regrets. Regrets that things weren't different. Regrets that there wouldn't be a tomorrow, even a tomorrow filled with the despair of homelessness was still a tomorrow. I go to sleep hoping that the mercy of sleep stole away their last thoughts too.

On April 11th the local newspaper reported that the individual had been identified "as that of a 50-year-old homeless man." Bailey (I'm protecting his name out of respect) is the man who tragically died underneath the overpass, and yes, Bailey was homeless. Thanks to the paper's staff writer, we also know approximately how many times Bailey had been picked up for public intox, where the majority of those offenses occurred, and even the year that he was first entered into the county's court system! This is outstanding work. But of course, you may remember this staff writer as the tabulator of homeless arrests from his report last year on our friend Rodney entitled – *"Homeless man found dead had been arrested 92 times."* Bailey, like Rodney, suffered from alcoholism and most of us understand this to be a disease that is exceedingly difficult to overcome, even for those with support systems in place. The Centers for Disease Control and Prevention reports that three in ten adults 18 years of age and over have had alcoholism and/or engaged in alcohol abuse at some point in their lives. Most people represented in those numbers however will never be at risk for public intox arrests or the humiliation of having them numbered in the local news because they have homes that conceal and protect them. People who do not have the luxury of a home and are victims of alcoholism are always at risk. And adding to the injury of the disease, they are also at constant risk of the insult and humiliation of those who perpetuate the dehumanizing stereotypes.

Writer and former Bishop of Edinburgh in the Scottish Episcopal Church, Richard Holloway in his book *Between the Monster and the Saint* says that "The human herd, when collectively aroused, is the most ferocious beast on the planet. It is responsible for every lynching, every act of genocide, every heresy hunt, and every ugly bout of group thinking that has ever afflicted the human community. Sadly, there always seem to be charismatic monsters around who are brilliant at rousing the herd and hypnotizing it into obedient servitude to their terrifying visions." Injuriously insulting a sick man in public (even after he is deceased), who has no way of privately wrestling with his illness, does not rise near to the level of a lynching or genocide, but it does help to arouse the herd that assumes the posture of criminalizing the homeless. Nor would I suggest that this staff writer and/or the newspaper he works for rise to the level of a monster, but they cannot be completely unaware of the damage they do when they continue to intentionally summarize the identity of homeless individuals by nothing more than quantifying their arrest reports.

We could of course give the staff writer the benefit of the doubt, maybe this is his assigned task at the newspaper. Maybe he's only following directions. Maybe he's been put in charge of reinforcing and promoting the homeless stereotypes. But regardless of who is actually responsible for generating these counts, they become both the mouthpiece of and the rallying cry for the herd whose damage it inflicts causes far more harm than just the embarrassing exposure of public name-calling. This propaganda brainwashes and gives birth to prejudices that effectively crystallize the community's willingness to see each one of these individuals as one like themselves – someone thrown into a unique and specific life context, the earliest stages of which had profound effects, for good or ill, on their subsequent history. We've all felt the frustration over an attack on our character or the consequences of an action being cast without being given the chance to explain ourselves – whether to a parent, friend, spouse, or boss. There's a reason for this, there's an explanation for that... "let me explain, please!" And to refuse to listen to an explanation, regardless of whether it may change one's mind, is completely unreasonable and often cruel. These prejudices then become part of the systemic forces that profile and keep people outside the structures of our community, like the refusal to consider a job applicant who doesn't have a permanent address.

I understand needing to fill space in a paper, feeling like you have to say *something*, and I don't know how much effort it took to gather the data on Rodney's or Bailey's arrest reports. Maybe not much at all. But I wonder how much more of an effort it would have taken to attempt to find out something about these two men as people. It would be nice to honor the deceased with the "chance to explain." I'm not a nimble researcher, but it took me about 15 minutes to uncover the fact that Bailey was the son of a Pentecostal Baptist Church pastor in Oneida, TN. He was a retired railroad trainman from the Brotherhood of Railroad Trainmen, and past president of the retired Railroaders Club. What I found particularly interesting was that the reverend passed away in 1982, *the very same year of Bailey's first entry into the County court system.* Now I won't presume a scenario without the facts to corroborate, but Bailey would have been about 21 years old when his father passed away and it wouldn't be too far-fetched to suggest the negative effect that it may have had on him, what support or guiding influence could have been lost. Whatever the case, with minimal exertion, this newspaper's readers may have been able to come away with a plausible explanation and kinder regard for the man that passed away tucked hopelessly underneath the overpass than what can be gained from a cold accounting of his arrests.

As I write, I am just learning of the body of 29-year-old Joshua (I'm protecting his name out of respect), a homeless person being found underneath the back porch of a local suburban home. The report is written by, you guessed it – the same staff writer. Stay tuned for Joshua's arrest report.

Finally, to Bailey. I don't know what unique and specific life context you were thrown into or the forces that came to visit you as you struggled to navigate this life, but I'd like the last words to ever run across a printing press in regard to your life and death to be kinder than the last.

Rest in peace.

Democratic Dictators

The idea that the majority rules, gives those numbered among the majority comfort, and those in the minority the hope that they may have a fighting chance. Sometimes the majority will do the right thing, but generally only when it is of benefit to them. If a community democratically elects to do the wrong thing – an unjust thing, then a democracy is no more admirable than a dictatorship that does the same. There is no honor in doing the wrong thing, simply because it has been dictated by the majority – in a 'democratic' way.

There are times when a community must be held accountable for doing the right thing, even when it contradicts the desires and demands of the majority. There are towns and cities all across the South that would still be fully segregated to this day, had those communities been allowed to wield 'the tyranny of the majority.' On September 23, 1957, police escorted nine African American children into Little Rock's all-white Central High School – against and in the face of an armed majority's will. Just over fifty years later, there can't be many people left who would dare suggest that the right thing wasn't done.

The French political thinker and historian, Tocqueville, wrote, "If it be admitted that a man possessing absolute power may misuse that power by wronging his adversaries, why should not a majority be liable to the same reproach? Men do not change their characters by uniting with one another; nor does their patience in the presence of obstacles increase with their strength. For my own part, I cannot believe it; the power to do everything, which I should refuse to one of my equals, I will never grant to any number of them." Tyranny of the Majority, Chapter XV, Book 1, Democracy in America. The evils of injustice can be just as easily wrought by the hands of a democracy as by a tyrannical dictator.

In the city and county's new efforts to solicit the mainstream community's input on how to address homelessness, we must be committed to doing the right thing, even if it runs contrary to the majority's will. We must resist the idea that we are seeking the welfare of the community, for there are two communities – we who live inside the margins, and those who've been pushed beyond. When we in the mainstream hide behind the suggestion that we are pursuing what's best for our community, what we really mean is what's best for us – what can we do with those who are homeless to make things better for us. A democracy that distinguishes itself from a dictatorship must guarantee that the majority will not abuse its power to violate the basic and inalienable rights of the minority. The minority's rights must be protected no matter how singular or alienated that minority is from the majority society, otherwise, the majority's rights lose their meaning. James Madison, alluding to slavery, wrote, "It is of great importance in a republic, not only to guard the society against the oppression of its rulers but to guard one part of the society against the injustices of the other part."

Only when we seek a solution that genuinely pursues the welfare of *their* community can we say that we are doing the right thing. Only when we seek a solution that mends the torn fabric of our two communities can we cultivate peace. And only when we see the day that a homeless shelter is as foreign to us as a water fountain labeled, "for whites only," can we say that we have surpassed compassion and achieved justice.

Reflecting and Mapping our Trajectory

Every November I turn another year older. And on that certain day, I will schedule some time to constructively reflect on the past year of my life, (providing it doesn't conflict with my drifting into some melancholic trance). I think it's important to live one's life with an outward-facing posture – that after it's all said and done, not only will I have become a better person, but the world would be a better place for my having been here. There are events in our lives that interrupt our regularly scheduled programs and force us to stop, take inventory, and adjust. But birthdays are those scheduled, gentle rest stops that require you to be intentional about reflection. There is usually no eventful episode that requires your response, and if you allow, the day will pass without your having considered these things at all.

As time goes by, you become increasingly aware of missed opportunities, and dwelling in the past is pointless and paralyz-ing, but looking back at your past with a purpose can make all the difference in the world. Not only can we avoid repeating bad decisions, but we can also trace the trajectory of our lives and determine where we will most likely be in the years to come. We're not hostages of these trajectories, but adjusting their course may sometimes require a "firing of the engines." I'm reminded of the film *Apollo 13* and the nerve-wracking ride the astronauts endured for those few seconds when the engines were fired to correct the ship's trajectory. These decisions can produce a wild ride, but they may be a necessary one in order to "get home."

Every November this paper turns another year older as well, and so I am thinking back on not only this past year but the two years this month marks. I like to think that the paper has provided our community with something of a "firing of the engines" – an adjustment in the trajectory of how we look at the issue of homelessness, its causes, and cures as well as providing an insider's look at the lives of our homeless neighbors. As we advocate on behalf of those experiencing homelessness, we stand in solidarity with these neighbors of ours and assume an outward-facing posture that seeks to inspire our community toward taking up a more sensitive and better-informed approach in its strategies to end homelessness. It's been a wild ride, and if we consider the trajectory of the program itself, we have only a two-year line to analyze, but we believe it's been worth the hours of hard work in contributing to our community's efforts of "getting home" on this issue. Our first year was an uncharted experiment, but at the close of our second, we like the trajectory. Homelessness can be such a polarizing issue, and we have our opponents, but the overwhelming support that we have enjoyed (and if you are reading this, you are most likely numbered among them) combined with a number of our vendors gaining meaningful employment and the fourteen who can now be referred to as "formerly homeless" goes a long way in affirming the direction we're going.

That direction? Well, if our trajectory is correct, our final destination is a time and place where a homeless street paper has no use, and the sooner we get there, the better.

Our intention is to make this a better community for us *having been* here and although I'll be very thankful to make it to another November, I'd be just as thankful if this paper doesn't.

The Shame We Feel

Whatever the opinions and degree of education of a man of today, whatever his shade of liberalism, whatever his school of philosophy, or of science or of economics, however ignorant or superstitious he may be, every man of the present day knows that all men have an equal right to life and the good things of life, and that one set of people are no better nor worse than another, that all are equal. Yet at the same time everyone sees all around him the division of men into two castes – the one, laboring, oppressed, poor, and suffering, the other idle, oppressing, luxurious, and profligate. And everyone not only sees this, but voluntarily or involuntarily, in one way or another, he takes part in maintaining this distinction which his conscience condemns. And he cannot help suffering from the consciousness of this contradiction and his share in it."

These words by Tolstoy are timeless in their application – they tell of a basic principle that, if we're honest, we all recognize. Namely, that something is just not right about a society or community where there is so much disparity in not only "the good things of life," but even of the things in life that are required in order to exist from day to day. And he is also accurate in saying that (at least most of us) recognize this and it bothers our conscience. Tolstoy was of course writing in opposition to the brutality and oppression of the Russian ruling class and the vast gulf that lay between them and the working class. In the context of our work here, it's hard to believe that we in the mainstream don't feel twinges of discomfort when we are confronted with the homeless in our community.

Our solutions to the uneasiness are either to remove the images or justify the disparity in privilege and prosperity. I don't think anyone would suggest that they don't feel uneasy when passing by a homeless person, whether it's only one while waiting at the end of an exit ramp or the many who pass the day around "the mission district." There may be cleverly crafted reasons given for the removal of the homeless from our streets and sidewalks, but you would have a difficult time convincing me that the primary catalyst does not lie somewhere in shame we feel when our eyes meet. For many years, to my shame, I would refuse to look. I couldn't. I would actually pull off the interstate, spot the homeless person, and immediately pretend as though I'm engaged in some operation within my car, so delicate, that it required my full attention. All the while, hoping and praying that he/she wouldn't approach my window and interrupt an expression on my face as though I was attempting to split an atom, only to catch me fast-forwarding through a cassette tape. It wasn't that I didn't want to give, it was that when our eyes met, I would be arrested by paralysis of a more deep-seated shame.

And then there are the others – much, much smaller in number I hope, who really have managed to convince themselves that the person holding the cardboard sign has no one to blame but him or herself for their predicament. There are certainly some cases when this is true, not everyone has a safety net, but through making that eye contact and engaging, many of us will come to see that the broad-sweeping assumption that this is the case, even more often than not, is simply *not* the case. We want to appeal to the level playing field that we've created. However, the more time you spend among the homeless, the more you'll come to appreciate the fact that yes, we may all be playing on a level playing field – same length, width, etc., but we have not all had access to the same quality coaching, the same equipment, and tools, the same degree of connectivity that keeps someone in the game rather than on the bench, regardless of their qualifications, or the same level of encouraging fan support.

I really don't have a solution for the dilemma at the end of the ramp or the painful and sometimes shocking drive through the mission district, but I would suggest this – that we surrender our attempts at trying to hide and justify homelessness and begin facing not only the issue but the people suffering behind the issue. By keeping these reminders of where we fail at community always before us, we may one day be driven towards finding the solutions for the real and shameful dilemma behind our dilemma.

It Was Not the Cause, But the Result

It is not for kings, O Lemuel,
it is not for kings to drink wine,
or for rulers to strong drink;
or else they will drink and forget what has been decreed,
and will pervert the rights of all the afflicted.
Give strong drink to one who is perishing,
and wine to those in bitter distress;
let them drink and forget their poverty,
and remember their misery no more.
Speak out for those who cannot speak,
for the rights of all the destitute.
Proverbs 31.4-9

Poverty is a relative term. But there exists poverty of such a degree, regardless of the context or standard, that is not in keeping with the way life is meant to be. It is not a thing that had to be argued to a conclusion – there is an inherent awareness that dictates this objective truth to us. We know this whether we experience it, witness it, or imagine it. And it is a dark reality that we would all like to remove from our site, our conscience, and our lives. This is not the poverty of having less of the luxuries and pleasures that are enjoyed in an affluent society – those things that whet our appetites for more and breed frustration when we can't get them, those things that we erroneously insist are available to all with a little application of earnestness of effort. We're all fairly comfortable with justifying this sort of disparity – some have more, some have less, we all move on. The poverty that unnerves us, and rightly so, is the lack of those things that are essential to the wholeness and wellness of life, things like nutritious food to eat, a home to retreat to and flourish in (not to be confused with an emergency shelter), the opportunity to engage in work and creativity, to interact meaningfully in community. Very few people, regardless of their piety, ever elect to take a vow of this degree of poverty. Poverty of this degree is not to be desired and demands to be chased out of our minds. In a world so advanced in so many ways, there just seems to be no justification for it. Those who live in it have their ways of chasing it out of their minds, and those who don't but who may be exposed to its images and/or who live with the fears that it may be only a paycheck away for them, or who fear that they may even contribute to systems that create and reinforce this degree of poverty, have their ways.

Much of our substance abuse issues have to do with the chasing of hopelessness out of our minds, and figures from the latest HMIS report help to bear this out in regard to those experiencing homelessness. It is often assumed that substance abuse is one of the major contributing factors in causing one to fall into homelessness, and if that were true, we might conclude that for most of our homeless neighbors, their plight is self-inflicted. However, the latest figures report that only about 12% of those experiencing homelessness attribute it to substance abuse. Many of our homeless neighbors who struggle with substance abuse will tell you that it was not the cause, it is the result. They'll also tell you that it is not a satisfying alternative to the good life that most of us live. One can rightly argue the accumulative destruction brought on by substance abuse and no one knows that better than those of us who've been or are enslaved to it. But what is hard for some of us to relate to is the fact that without hope, the future does not exist, only the present. And so what can be done to alleviate the pain and misery of the present? I've asked many of our friends to sit with me and dream a dream for their lives – anything, regardless of how far out of reach or impossible to ever realize it may be. The most recent response came back, "A place to call home and food on the table." Really?! "Well, you said no matter how far out of reach it may be. Anyway, that's what I hope for."

The contents of our hope can seem small and lacking in imagination, but its power to transform our lives – to cause us to care about the present and engage the future is immeasurable. As our city begins its work on re-addressing the radical poverty of homelessness, we should not underestimate this power of hope. The strategies will be crucial but articulating and demonstrating well the sense of priority and urgency that we give to this epidemic can create a culture of hope that will breathe life into our efforts and give us the best chance to succeed.

We Do Not Want to Try
This Experiment

Occasionally I read or hear of the criticisms directed towards churches and faith-based organizations – that their good intentions only exasperate the aggravation that our neighborhoods have to endure from the homeless community. Now, we need to love our neighborhoods well. As a local minister and organizing leader based in Fort Sanders, I am particularly sensitive to neighborhoods being neglected, abused, and increasingly encroached upon. Fort Sanders is over ninety percent rental properties that are owned and operated in large part by absentee landlords who have no real vested interest in the care of the neighborhood. What makes matters worse is that most of these renters are students who are transient and whose care for the neighborhood is understandably fleeting at best. Add to this the perception from those few who have for years loved and called the Fort their home, that the University and the hospital are increasingly careless in their encroachments, and you have a neighborhood that barely fits the definition.

I will gladly go on record in defense of the Northside neighborhood's concerns for what seems to be a growing encroachment upon them by homeless service providers. We certainly don't need fewer service providers, but we do need to find ways to discourage them from congregating at the front door of one neighborhood. But I will also go on record in defense of the churches and the nonprofits who work among the homeless. We do get things wrong, for example, we often exhaust our efforts on feeding and clothing while failing to advocate for systemic changes; some of us, unfortunately, place prerequisites of being preached at in order to receive gifts; and then there's the damning insinuations of the correlating relationship between faith and prosperity, but the community at large would experience nothing short of anarchy without us. I mean, can you imagine the state of our cities across the country if the faith-based community adopted a "hands-off" approach to the homeless and marginalized? We do not want to try that experiment. And it's foolish to think that we'd be better off without these efforts 'cause "then they'd all be forced to get jobs."

If we're gonna criticize the churches and the nonprofits, then let's at least do so with the understanding that they will never be able to bring about the systemic changes that are required in solving the problem of homelessness. And this is where I, as a minister and nonprofit leader, have my peaceful nature challenged. It is up to our city, state, and national civic leaders to address these systemic injustices and stop relying on the luxury of time that these caring organizations provide by soothing the pain and meaninglessness of life on the streets. It's true what they say, "The squeaking wheel gets the grease" and it's easy to get the feeling that as long as we are there to suppress the squeaking, then our civic leaders can be busy about greasing other matters. In spite of the many ways in which we "enable" the homeless (other's words), we do at least create a context within which our communities ought to be able to address the roots of the issue. This is where the criticisms can be particularly irritating – it is not the responsibility of the churches and the nonprofits to hold the disenfranchised at bay indefinitely.

Contrary to popular belief, most of us are not in this for the money: it is the conscription of our conscience to do the right thing, in hopes that one day soon homeless service providers will be able to turn their attention to other matters. I have hopes that the city is moving in good directions, and that we are cultivating a community that wants to do the right thing- but there is a long way to go.

I assure you though, that regardless of all the criticisms we deserve, you do not want us to resign just yet.

To Die Another Day

I was talking with a member of our homeless community, and she expressed in one sentence what I had been struggling with for days during these weeks of extreme cold temperatures – that our community's response is a mixed bag of thankfulness and anger. "Where's all this concern any and every other time of the year!" Our thoughts were the same, but my struggle was ideological, hers were real. And her feelings represent the feelings of the community that is subjected to these confusing pendulum swings – from being harassed and swept beyond the margins, to being swept up into the rescuing arms of Jesus, (depending on the weather. Literally).

There's a heightened sense of urgency when there are people at risk of literally freezing to death, and I can see how my friend aches at the thought of her slow and agonizing death that is at work every other day of the year and yet goes virtually unnoticed. Or noticed but ignored. It's like the person who knows their diet is leading to heart disease, but only takes action upon having a heart attack. The doctors plead for a change, but there's always the sense that I'll address that later, or we just don't have the willpower to make those needed changes. Our communities take on a steady diet of systemic oppression against the homeless, some of it direct and intentional, most of it is the sense that it's just not a pressing concern for us or we just don't possess the willpower to make the needed changes, that is until our own personal guilt and shame are at stake. And this doesn't address those who are totally unaware that there is a problem.

There are too many people who are not aware of the systemic issues that contribute to and crystallize members of our communities in homelessness. And it is not overstating the crisis to say that these issues can contribute to the slow and painful death of people without homes. We memorialize them every year. Of course, we have the power to change these issues, but an appreciation for the need for change won't come if we're not made aware of the effects they have. And after having been made aware, we must address these very systemic issues rather than applying the endlessness of charity. Charity is always the mode of operation for some, and so the degree of need determines the degree, extent, and urgency of their response and involvement – like subfreezing weather calls for an "all hands on deck" approach. Unfortunately, many a charitable persons *and* organizations fail to appreciate the advantages of applying a sense of urgency in time and resources towards the systemic changes that can ultimately reduce the need for charity.

Change trumps (sorry, couldn't think of another term) charity every time.

And this is not a criticism of charitable acts or charitable people, they (we) are necessary. We need more Mother Teresas, But we also need more Dr. Kings – people who are working towards change. Contrary to what many may think, the general consensus within the homeless community is that they are weary of being the recipients of our charity, the objects of our ministries. No one knows the necessity of generosity as well as they do, particularly during the winter months. But this is the very thing that causes the confusing and opposing emotions within them - one of gratitude and thankfulness towards generous people, pitted against the anger and frustration of living in a society that seems bent on making their generosity necessary. It's a combination of a spoken, "thank you so much" and an under the breath, "can you please go away?!"

It's difficult, if not impossible for even the most disciplined of us to consistently sustain a sense of urgency, or a high level of consciousness and attention for just about anything, (even our own personal habits that we know are slowly killing us) but it's the wise person who tries. And change on any level will not come without trying. Bringing about systemic changes is hard work, vested interests of the unaffected are always there and ready to fight or "reason" us away. And quite honestly, it seems easier to rally an effort around collecting blankets than to work towards affordable housing and a living wage. And the dark side of me wonders if the good feeling one gets from extending charity is addictive to the point that it contributes to our lack of urgency to quench our thirst for it or even the organization's fear of working itself out of a job.

There are many homeless members of our community who are inexpressibly thankful that their neighbors have rallied around the urgent need of warmth and food this winter, but we neighbors must work towards systemic solutions, we must. It is inexcusable for a capable community to gin up enthusiastic generosity towards the homeless because of the immediacy of the moment, saving them only to die another day.

Delivering One Final, Meaningless, and Insulting Blow

On July 16th the body of Rodney (I'm protecting his name out of respect) was found in a field off Dale avenue. Rodney was a friend of mine, and I had the infuriating experience of seeing him identified by reading the report of a local newspaper's staff writer. Headline: *Homeless man found dead had been arrested 92 times.* The writer goes on to expose Rodney in shameful ways – ways that I will not repeat here. I thought this level of ignorance and disrespect was reserved for the comment section where people spew their venom anonymously, but it appears some are graduating to the staff.

Rodney was an alcoholic and most of us understand that to be a disease that is exceedingly difficult to overcome, even for those who have systems of support in place. The Centers for Disease Control and Prevention reports that three in ten adults 18 years of age and over have had alcoholism and/or engaged in alcohol abuse at some point in their lives. Most of those represented in those numbers however will never be at risk for public intox arrests because they have walls that hide and protect them. Rodney didn't have that luxury. Rodney lived outside and was always at risk, and if one cares to count, 92 times since 2006, but I can't imagine why someone wanted to count.

However, my contempt for his report goes far beyond the runaway stereotypes of the homeless as drunks that he carelessly fuels. No, what infuriates me is the absolute disregard for the intrinsic dignity of Rodney – a man. This day comes for all of us, and though only a few will be memorialized in print beyond our local obituary columns, I fail to see the purpose in exposing the worst in anyone in this way. Who comes up on a man beaten down to death and then runs up to deliver one final, meaningless, and insulting blow? What purpose can this possibly serve?

So that will not be the final words on my friend. As I remember Rodney, I remember a man who would go canning through the student-populated neighborhood. It used to be much easier when the local exchange would accept his cans, but now it is a long walk to Central Avenue. Rodney didn't complain though. When I would get frustrated over this difficulty on his behalf, he would settle me down with an appreciative smile. I remember in the summers he'd be tired and covered in sweat, in the winters, he'd be clothed like he was going ice fishing. I remember that he would often set his bag down and pull up a seat with me on the sidewalk to catch up and talk about better times. Better times in his past, and his hope for better times to come. Rodney was gentle, kind and so easy to talk with. He was a man that I could just sit with and not say a word – watching a world go by that would often break us out in simultaneous laughter. Every day that I step out of the church, my eyes will be drawn to the spot on the sidewalk where Rodney and I sat and had our last conversation.

When our day comes, I like to think that something, some-place, or someone should be better off for each of us having been here. I am better off for Rodney having been here.

Rodney was not a drunk... he was a person.

"Panhandlers Usually Spend It on Alcohol and Drugs"

"A few cents may seem very little to you. *However, it does more harm than good, especially to the panhandlers themselves because...*" And the first bullet point with two more to follow reads: "*Panhandlers usually use the money to buy alcohol and drugs.*"

There is a movement among a number of cities across the country to discourage people from giving money to panhandlers. As well thought out as the strategy seems to be, I seriously doubt that it has much chance for success. If we take the above bullet point and add it to the following two that were included on a public notice placed in the window of a local downtown business: *Giving panhandlers your spare change does not help them address the circumstances that put them on the street, and it may discourage them from seeking assistance from social service agencies,* and *local social service agencies can help people change their circumstances by providing full meals, shelter, clothing, health care, and employment services.* The argument appears to be logical, constructive, and convincing. However, not only are there considerable flaws in the argument, but the approach by using logic will not likely reach those who are most prone to give. Think of the young girl who falls in love with and pursues the young man whom her parents warn is no good. They may confront her with a very logical and persuasive argument – "He has long hair, tattoos, no ambition, no money, and he doesn't believe like we do." And yet she loves him still. It's true what Pascal said, "Love has its reasons that reason knows nothing of." There are too many in our community who so love the meaningfulness of that simple exchange with the radically poor stranger and are not going to be easily swayed by logical arguments – regardless of how persuasive they seem. In fact, these kinds of efforts may even fuel their resolve. Again, not totally unlike the girl who amps up her displays of love for her boyfriend precisely as a result of her parents' animated objections.

But even for those who appreciate a good argument, these do have fundamental flaws. To begin with, the idea that *most* use the money for drugs and alcohol is the same unsubstantiated stereotype that undermined the very thing that the argument claims the third bullet point was trying to achieve, namely, permanent supportive housing. Most of us remember our city's Ten Year Plan being shelved because of the noise that was being raised over placing these units in our neighborhoods because the homeless are drug addicts, alcoholics, and therefore dangerous. In other words, the irony of the argument is that the very thing it suggests that our local service providers can do was undone because of the initial premise that the whole argument is built upon – that most of them are drug addicts and alcoholics. There can no longer be any doubt that permanent supportive housing works when it comes to "changing their circumstances." But it will never have the chance if we refuse to let go of the stereotypes that hinder our progress.

Now, one's spare change certainly does not address the *circumstances that put them on the streets*, but neither do *full meals, shelter, clothing, and health care*. These are all acts of mercy intended to ease the raw and tragic experience of homelessness, and you'd be hard-pressed to find someone living this pitiful existence who wouldn't gladly exchange these acts of mercy and a few dollars here and there for the life that you and I live.

I think it's true that in every context, love wins. It may not make sense, it may operate on impulse rather than calculated thought, and reason may even tell us that it's not the advisable thing to do, but I have no doubt that in the end, small acts of love and kindness will persist in the human heart. There's always the risk that someone might do with a few dollars what you'd rather they not do, but then there's also the risk that someone might miss out on the profound communion of humanity that can be stirred by the exchange of those *few cents*.

It's Miller Time

So I'm having lunch with Wolfman, a homeless friend. He's all up in arms about his previous night's arrest for public intoxication, but he's even more incensed that his picture was plastered across a local paper the following day. What he said next stayed with me: "I guess now I'm the town drunk!" Now, aside from our instinct to immediately launch into a lecture that starts with something like "Well, that's what you get for..." from those of us whose behavioral record still reads undefeated (or with an asterisk noting that our defeats were only mistakes, not indications of deeper-seated flaws like those of the poor), you might be a little surprised that a homeless man even cares about his reputation. And that can reveal a stereotype that most of us in the mainstream hold towards the homeless in general – that they're so morally bereft of basic human values, that they've even lost all sensitivity of having guilt or shame. My initial thought was, "You know, man, the only thing you're guilty of is not having a golf course, a boat, or a backyard patio, a county club, a frat house, or a political function, to get drunk at."

This is not, by the way, a rant against the laws regarding public intoxication, but against the stigma attached to the behavior of a homeless person who's had too much to drink, that casts a stereotype on all those who don't have the luxury of concealing their behavior behind the insulation of our social structures. For example, when it comes to allowing the formerly homeless to drink in the privacy of their own homes, we hear that it's "a slippery slope." And the matter of how it may be subsidized is a non-related issue. These sentiments alone insinuate that "these people" are not comprised of the same strength of moral fiber as we in the mainstream are. When students get drunk, they're just doing what students do. When the working class gets drunk, they're just blowing off a day's hard work, embodying the old commercial that announces, "It's Miller Time!" When businessmen or our elected officials get drunk, they're just christening alliances and relieving stress. Even those who struggle with alcoholism are afforded the appropriate decency of sympathy for an uninvited disease. But none of the above groups are going to bear the mainstream assessment as being morally deficient because of their behavior. They are protected by one another's mutual acceptance and leniency. Their excess is not perceived as having an adverse effect on the community. Their slippery slope has a cushioned landing. The homeless are not included in this unspoken agreement that the rest of us have with one another. A homeless man who has had more than the legal limit mandates is not only labeled a drunk, but he also bears the weight of every other characterization that comes with the package of assumptions we make about him, based on the initial premise that he is morally and ethically bankrupt.

Contrary to our assumptions, the homeless in our community share the same values that you and I in the mainstream are believed to hold. Their seemingly divergent behavior is the result of a number of things, but primarily their radical existence, and their need to survive against forces too raw and hopeless for most of us to even imagine. Their bitterness towards a society that lives a comfortable world apart from them can cause them to show outward signs that appear to reject that same society's core values. They can even reach the point where our labels, our glares, and our policies aimed against them can fuel self-fulfilling prophecies. All of this is not to say that they don't still hold the same values we do. Rather, it's more accurate to say that they lose all interest in putting them on display for us – to please us, to impress us, to convince us that they're deserving of our help. We shouldn't assume, then, that their behavior, nor ours, is necessarily the product of values.

For example, how many apologies begin with an explanatory phrase like "I'm sorry, I'm just really tired..." or "I'm just really frustrated with ..."? These phrases lose all their thrust, all their meaning, if we don't really believe that the circumstances, they convey excuse or exonerate the divergent behavior that we claim they cause.

The point is, we often attribute our behavior to the forces around us, the forces we often claim are beyond our control. And so, once again, we in the mainstream enjoy an allegiance that allows for the divergence of conduct that the homeless, or radically underprivileged, aren't welcome to join. If we justify our temporary divergences based upon our temporary circumstances of discomfort, frustration, etc. then what can we expect from those for whom these similar circumstances are a way of life? There comes a point in time when one is tired of saying, "I'm sorry." There should also come a point in time when others can say, "I didn't know, and I too am sorry." If we in the mainstream can make the effort to abandon these baseless assumptions toward the underprivileged and homeless, then genuine and holistic community healing can find a place to spread roots and grow. The way forward is long and difficult, not just for one group or another, but for all, and it must begin, and continue, with dignity, compassion, and understanding.

They Have Surrendered
To It

I'm thinking about this word, "enabling" that I hear occasionally in the context of how we within the margins interact with
those outside, (figuratively and literally). I can't help but believe
that some of our preconceived notions about the homeless help
to fuel the ease with which we use the word. That, and perhaps
the license it gives us to do the bare minimum – or nothing at
all – under the guise of being responsible.

I think some of us must start with the notion that most of
the homeless in our community have chosen this lifestyle, and
therefore we have an obligation to help make their lives so miserable that we literally drive them off the streets. In other words, to
do something for a homeless person that would give them some
degree of pleasure or comfort only "enables" their choosing to
continue in this lifestyle. Without hesitation, I can say that I have
never known a single one out of the many, who would not have
traded places with me in an instant. There are certainly those
who struggle to function well in our society (there are days that
I could number myself among them) and choose to live in some

sense outside it. But to suggest that this characterizes the homeless community as a whole is simply not true. It is also a fact that there are some among the homeless community who have all but given up on reintegration and find it pointless and demoralizing to summon the energy to try and work something that seems to be systematically set against them. But again, this doesn't mean that they have chosen this lifestyle – more accurately, they have surrendered to it.

When it comes to providing meals, for example, there is often the idea that we promote homelessness by offering anything more than what is required to keep one from starving. There are actually movements among a number of U.S. cities that are indirectly aimed at outlawing providing the homeless with food at all. According to a report released by The National Coalition for the Homeless and The National Center on Homelessness, from Myrtle Beach to San Diego, cities both large and small are pursuing restrictions on who can feed, how many can you feed, and at what times, and how often can the homeless be fed. Cities are attempting to prohibit "unauthorized" people by the uncertified public, to feed the homeless. Proponents of the ordinances claim that they will, among other things, ensure the safety of the food given to the homeless. Do we have, "unable to see through you" written across our foreheads? Thankfully, these cities are the exception rather than the rule. However, it is a very common assumption across most if not all of our communities that providing the homeless with good food on a regular basis is irresponsible and will only affirm their conclusion that sleeping in the mud and snow is great.

I sometimes think that operating under our preconceived notions – that the homeless have chosen this lifestyle because they're lazy drunks and drug addicts – we feel guilty if we do something that brings a smile to their faces. That they have no business being happy, have no business being excused through our extravagant offerings from reflecting on the shame they should feel for choosing such an existence. It's easy to perpetuate these feelings when we see the homeless as no more than the objects of our charity.

"When I feed the poor, they call me a saint, but when I ask why the poor are hungry, they call me a communist" Dom Helder Camara

Should Having a Home Depend On Someone's Profit?

Poet and philosopher Eli Siegel was the first to ask the question, "What does a person deserve by being alive?"

How can we continue to live with the shame of building, sustaining, and even celebrating societies that arrogantly refuse to recognize the inalienable right of every human being born into this world to have a home? We have become so mesmerized by our dominating systems of profit and oppression, that we have lost all ability to reference the simplicity of what we as humans ought to be able to access outside another man's will, and that is a home, our daily bread and to love and be loved.

"The fundamental question about housing...is: should a person make a profit from the need of another person to have a home, shelter, a place to live? Should our ability to have a home depend on whether we can provide a profit for somebody?" Ellen Reiss.

Who'll deny that money is always the root of our evils? Karl Marx once wrote that "Money is the universal, self-constituted value of all things. It has therefore robbed the whole world, human as well as natural, of its own values. Money is the alienated essence of man's work and being. This alien essence dominates him, and he adores it."

We are in fact so indebted to the systems that hold out promises of wealth that we can actually assuage the guilt of seeing people wander the streets by casting the blame on them. We defend the systems that oppress like a child sides with the school bully in hopes that his loyalty will earn him favor and security. But the bully really doesn't give a damn about anyone and can just as easily and capriciously turn on his adherents in an instant and without warning, leaving them with no other recourse but to beg for re-admittance.

Most of us in the mainstream take for granted the help we received upon entering this world. We didn't *earn* a family that taught us and demonstrated to us how to 'make it in this world.' We didn't *earn* a family that had the economic resources to empower our endeavors. We didn't *earn* a family with the connectivity or clout to bail us out of the troubles we get ourselves into that would cripple those without. We didn't *earn* the mental or physical capacity that might enable us to engage and pursue what our systems require in order to experience the wholeness and wellness of life.

Yes, people do overcome hurdles, but it is the exception that anyone should ever overcome being ill-equipped from the start to achieving any real degree of functional stability. That's why we love success stories- because they are so exceptional, almost miraculous. Not to mention the fact that they also help to re-inforce our 'feel good' myth that anyone can make it in this society if they just try hard enough.

Here's an experiment for you. Sit down with 5 or 6 of your friends to a game of monopoly. Give them all varying amounts of money, properties, houses, hotels, etc. and you start with nothing – not even the instructions. See how well you do. To make the experiment additionally realistic, (and demoralizing), take note of how those around the table begin to determine your worth and your deservedness for their help accordingly.

Good luck.

As Herbert Gans wrote, "Changing behavior is always more productive than changing attitudes. But when the law and the economy are not available to change behavior, we must be satis-fied with changing attitudes and hope that these may have some impact on behavior."

I hope that we all open our minds and hearts to a change in our attitudes this side of homelessness. I assure you that once you need the experience of homelessness to change it for you... this world will no longer be yours and you will have lost all power to impact your community's behavior.

"The world should be owned by the people living in it... All persons should be seen as living in a world truly theirs." Eli Siegel.

Mistaking the Journey
for the Destination

Sometimes in life, due to our misguided efforts or our misguided intentions, we find ourselves mistaking the journey for the destination. Sometimes we can find ourselves seemingly unable, or unwilling to see beyond our community's efforts to relieve the raw and hopeless existence of our homeless neighbors – the charitable work we do, to see what should be the destination – empowerment and enfranchisement.

For some of us, the reason is simply that we love our charity. We love the feeling we get when we volunteer at a soup kitchen. This doesn't mean we are void of any feelings for the objects of our charity, (I long for the day when I no longer have to hear the term "the needy") nor would I suggest that we shouldn't feel some sense of rightness, but we can't allow the warmness of the experience to satisfy us in such a way that we don't climb inside our car, lean back, exhale and ask, "What is wrong here!" As long as we operate under the assumption that homelessness is a national and community disease with no cure, we will continue to misunderstand the true meaning of our charity.

As Martin Luther King Jr. said: "Our acts of compassion and charity are essential, but we cannot allow them to become the end in themselves." We must see them for what they are – our obligation to care for the casualties of a system that produces homelessness. "... On the one hand, we are called to play the Good Samaritan on life's roadside, but that will be only an initial act. One day we must come to see that the whole Jericho Road must be transformed so that men and women will not be constantly beaten and robbed as they make their journey on life's highway. True compassion is more than flinging a coin at a beggar. It comes to see that an edifice which produces beggars needs restructuring."

And this brings us to another reason that some of us confuse our charity with the destination – we refuse to acknowledge that the economic system so many of us benefit from does not work for everyone. And that in order for things to systematically change and for genuine democracy to break out, those who are disenfranchised will have to rise up and demand to be allowed into the mainstream. And this, quite honestly, frightens many of us. We don't intentionally purpose this, and we would never say it, but there are many of us who subconsciously prefer to feed and clothe the homeless rather than see them mobilized and empowered to stand shoulder to shoulder with the rest of us in places of power and decision. This is what was behind Marx's assertion that "religion is the opiate of the masses." This was not as much a commentary on religion, as much as it was a commentary on how societies can systematically medicate their oppressed and underprivileged to the point where they are co-matose and incapable of waking up and realizing even a need for change, much less summon the strength to fight for it. Unless we the many across this community who are engaged in works of charity and compassion are intentional in our efforts to see it as the sustenance needed to awaken, energize, and strengthen with a view towards its destination – empowerment, and not just what is required to see them through another day, our homeless community can easily find itself drawn towards our charity as their destination itself.

When we in the mainstream, together with the marginalized, view charity as the destination, rather than the fuel for empower-ment, the reality of ending homelessness will remain a fantasy for the one and a dream for the other.

"...So They Can Live a Productive Life"

On February 9ᵗʰ, both city and county mayors announced via press conference that the Ten-Year Plan to End Chronic Homelessness was being "reset" to seek more community input. We were told that the plan would be "tweaked;" starting with the naming of a new committee to study the plan. With the announcement, came the resignation of the TYP Director and the assistant for communications and funding. While the rumors are rampant, the reason for these changes is unknown. It takes a fair amount of optimism to conclude that February 9 marked anything but the end of the Ten-Year Plan to End Chronic Homelessness. On the heels of that day's announcement we then heard suggestions that the strategy of whatever is to follow, may not include permanent supportive housing as a component. If this should happen to be the case, then the Ten-Year Plan, or whatever new name it may take on, is surely destined for a suffocating end. I don't know how we could even let that suggestion enter the conversation. Would we ever suggest a strategy to address our community's food injustices without food as a component of the solution?

I can see the pieces on the board moving toward an endless stalemate. It's one thing to get caught up in the debate on how best to implement permanent supportive housing, but if the "step back" we're taking is to place us into a debate on its very relevance, then we may as well get comfortable. What ultimately makes these kinds of debates excruciatingly fruitless is that they are always argued by and from the perspectives of those outside the group they're intended to benefit. It was promising to hear that the new committee will include people who are formerly homeless. Whether or not those voices are heard remains to be seen. I would challenge the powers that be to ask at least one currently homeless person to be on the committee. Even those of us who consider ourselves to be the most committed advocates rarely engage from a perspective of any real identifiable experience. I think about the current healthcare problems in America and easily conclude that if our elected officials, along with the others profiting from the industry, were all making about $30,000 a year and having to buy their own insurance, these problems would have been resolved 20 years ago. Our profits and our morals just can't seem to get along. Unless, of course, we define our morals by our profits. This is how we begin to determine a person's worth – by their ability to earn and produce. I recall hearing one of the mayors conclude a sentence in the press conference that was intended to indicate the goal of our efforts to house the homeless: "...so that they can live productive lives."

To begin with, a human being deserves the security of a home regardless of their productivity. As a result of one's intrinsic worth, one ought to have the intrinsic right to a dignified place to call home. But this statement also reveals our ongoing loss of focus on the ones the TYP was intended to address – the chronically homeless. By definition, these members of our community may never be in a position to live a productive life. At least not in the sense that would satisfy most in the mainstream as "pulling their weight." And then, of course, beyond the challenges of being able to agree upon financial solutions, our morals have to battle the perceived threats to health, home, and happiness. In other words, we'll feed and clothe the homeless as long as we can keep them safely away from us. Even an optimist could find it difficult to imagine any solution to the chronically homeless not being held in check by a combination of these and other yet-to-be-determined obstacles. And I understand that our city considers itself a compassionate city, but unless our compassion actually drives us to house the chronically homeless, that claim loses all validity. This is first and foremost a matter of basic human rights, and all other matters must get in line. It is time for our collective conscience to wake up and be the driving force behind finding these solutions. It must also be the force which determines the pace at with we work towards them. It is not an over-dramatization to say that lives are in the balance as we push the reset button on the process.

Nothing happens collectively that doesn't happen individually first. So we call upon the individuals across this community to rise up and give this moral imperative the strength it needs to battle through the thickets of economic fixations and unfounded prejudices, to demand that this process move forward with a sense of equity as well as urgency.

Home: The Challenge

From the moment we're born, life is a struggle, and no one emerges self-sufficient. The extent to which we will survive, much less flourish in life is hugely determined by those who provide, teach, protect, and mentor us throughout our early years and stages. We don't earn these things, they are the influential people, communities, organizations, and structures that we are born into and raised in the midst of – all by no choosing of our own. Our ultimate success in life is then also hugely determined by the measure of success of these influences in our lives to both equip us with tools needed, show us how they work, and to instill in us the determination to use them. The time then comes for most of us when we have to venture out from the safety and security of these support structures and 'make it' on our own. Even once the training wheels come off, most of us will have had a parent who ran alongside us, helping us to steady ourselves while providing the confidence needed that if we should lose our balance, we would be caught. I really believe that this describes best the idea that President Obama was trying to convey in his infamous, "...you didn't build it" statement. Those words have infuriated many Americans, and I believe that much of it has to do with our fear that if we ever should admit that the success in our lives has in fact been largely afforded us by resources and influences beyond our control, then we can't justify pronouncing judgment on those who have lived in generations of poverty. No one wants to live a life where they feel as though they have no or little control over their outcome, but for many, this is in fact the raw truth. And those of us in stations of privilege who refuse to acknowledge that, only sow seeds of bitterness and provoke further the ideas of class warfare.

I was having a conversation with one of our volunteers this past week and was once again confronted with how her reality is so embodied in the lives of many of those in our community experiencing homelessness, and how it can actually quench any desire to escape the streets. Out of homelessness for only three months now, my friend's will to keep trying nearly collapses. "I had it easier on the streets. At least I had a little money for food." My friend is working part-time at a fast-food restaurant and trying to pay $600.00 rent in a roach-infested apartment out east. Two-thirds Cherokee and growing up on a reservation-like environment, her challenges have been formidable from the start. She's made mistakes as we all do, and because of one that's labeled her a felon, (not everyone has the privileged connections that turn felonious actions into harmless misdemeanors) she is not likely to get housing assistance to help create space in her budget for food, clothing, and the pursuit of furthering her education. The desire is there, but the current structures and the effects of her underprivileged past cause her to conclude that the ship bearing those good things in life has sailed.

She's the child who never had the training wheels, nor the watchful and attentive parent to run alongside her. She bears the scars and the pain from many unprotected falls and is quickly losing the confidence and will to climb back on.

We say that the solution to homelessness is housing, and of course, it is. But surely housing should be more than the object of one's dreams or the contributor to their struggles. Home should be the safe and secure place in which one casts their dreams outward while providing the stability to reach and achieve those dreams with the confidence of a child breezing down the street, riding "no hands" and grinning from ear to ear.

I assure her that all's not lost, don't give up, and that it's never too late.

And I return to my office, close my eyes, and hope that I've told her the truth.

Acknowledgments

I owe my thoughts, perspectives, positions, and opinions that are expressed in this book to the members of the homeless community that I've had the privilege to share life with over the past ten years. You inspired and shaped me. You welcomed me into your space, and there is no one that I would rather have had in mine.